Vegetation Community Monitoring at Cape Lookout National Seashore, 2010

Natural Resource Report NPS/SECN/NRDS—2012/258

Michael W. Byrne and Sarah L. Corbett

USDI National Park Service
Southeast Coast Inventory and Monitoring Network
Cumberland Island National Seashore
101 Wheeler Street
Saint Marys, Georgia, 31558

and

Joseph C. DeVivo

USDI National Park Service
Southeast Coast Inventory and Monitoring Network
University of Georgia
160 Phoenix Road, Phillips Lab
Athens, Georgia, 30605

March 2012

U.S. Department of the Interior
National Park Service
Natural Resource Stewardship and Science
Fort Collins, Colorado

The National Park Service, Natural Resource Stewardship and Science office in Fort Collins, Colorado publishes a range of reports that address natural resource topics of interest and applicability to a broad audience in the National Park Service and others in natural resource management, including scientists, conservation and environmental constituencies, and the public.

The Natural Resource Data Series is intended for the timely release of basic data sets and data summaries. Care has been taken to assure accuracy of raw data values, but a thorough analysis and interpretation of the data has not been completed. Consequently, the initial analyses of data in this report are provisional and subject to change.

All manuscripts in the series receive the appropriate level of peer review to ensure that the information is scientifically credible, technically accurate, appropriately written for the intended audience, and designed and published in a professional manner.

This report received informal peer review by subject-matter experts who were not directly involved in the collection, analysis, or reporting of the data.

Data in this report were collected and analyzed using methods based on established, peer-reviewed protocols and were analyzed and interpreted within the guidelines of the protocols.

Views, statements, findings, conclusions, recommendations, and data in this report do not necessarily reflect views and policies of the National Park Service, U.S. Department of the Interior. Mention of trade names or commercial products does not constitute endorsement or recommendation for use by the U.S. Government.

This report is available from (http://science.nature.nps.gov/im/units/secn) and the Natural Resource Publications Management website (http://www.nature.nps.gov/publications/nrpm/).

Please cite this publication as:

Byrne, M. W., S. L. Corbett, and J. C. DeVivo. 2012. Vegetation community monitoring at Cape Lookout National Seashore, 2010. Natural Resource Data Series NPS/SECN/NRDS—2012/258. National Park Service, Fort Collins, Colorado.

NPS 623/112986, March 2012

Contents

Figures

Tables

List of Terms

Absolute cover: The total amount of ground surface that is covered by each species or group. Describes the amount of cover that each species or group represents in a stratum. Expressed as a percentage. Can exceed 100% due to overlap. The total cover of each species or group divided by the total possible cover for a plot.

Canopy species: Woody species known to occur in the midstory or overstory of the canopy, or shrub species that grow greater than or equal to 4 cm DBH and measureable at breast height (1.4 m).

Canopy stratum: The structural zone above 1.1 m (i.e., elbow height of a typical observer as per densiometer instructions) and consists of all live and dead plant material that affects the amount of light penetrating to the ground. This includes individual elements whose cover is also potentially measured and accounted for in the shrub- or groundcover-stratum measurements, but exceeds 1.1 m in height, is detected by the densiometer, and contributes to canopy cover. Also referred to as the midstory, overstory, or sub-canopy.

Cover: The vertical projection of the outermost extent of a species, or the extent of the shadow cast by the species if the sun were directly overhead. Foliar cover.

DBH: Diameter at breast height, or 1.4 m above the ground's surface.

Frequency: The number of times a species or group is detected in a plot, expressed as a percentage. Provides information on regularity at which a species or group is encountered.

Groundcover stratum: The structural zone that consists of all non-woody species (i.e., forbs and graminoids), and all woody species (i.e., shrubs and trees) with a DBH of less than 1 cm and seedlings 30 cm or less in height.

Relative cover: The cover of each species or group as a function of all other plant species that occurred in a plot. Describes the percentage of cover that each species represents out of the total vegetative cover in a stratum. Expressed as a percentage. Always sums to 100%. The total cover of each species or group divided by the sum of the cover of all other species that occur in a plot.

Seedlings: Woody dicotyledonous plants less than 30 cm in height.

Shrub stratum: All woody species greater than 30 cm in height with a DBH of 1–4 cm.

Stratum: A structural size category of vegetation at a site. These are the canopy, shrub, and groundcover layers.

Executive Summary

In 2009, the National Park Service (NPS) Southeast Coast Network (SECN) Inventory and Monitoring Network began collecting plant community data as part the NPS Vital Signs monitoring program. Information collected under this Vital Sign will be used to help managers make better informed decisions by understanding trends and variability related to plant species, frequency of occurrence, percent cover, diversity, and distribution in the groundcover, shrub, and canopy strata.

Within each stratum, plant communities were sampled using a hybrid of methods used by the North Carolina Vegetation Survey nested-subplot design (Peet et al. 1998) within a circular plot similar to the Forest Inventory and Analysis protocol (Bechtold and Patterson 2005). This report summarizes plant community data collected at Cape Lookout National Seashore in 2010.

1. Data were collected at 30 spatially-balanced random locations at the Seashore. The findings below apply only to portions of the park that meet the following site selection criteria:

    a) Sites are located within park boundaries and ownership.

    b) Sites must be sampleable within safety guidelines.

    c) Sites cannot be located in wholly non-natural areas, open water, or areas where application of the methods is inappropriate (such as marshes).

2. Sampling activities occurred at the Seashore from 7/12 to 8/3/2010

3. Monitoring efforts resulted in the addition of 14 species, subspecies, and varieties to the park's species list.

4. Absolute canopy cover across the park was approximately 11%.

5. Virginia live oak (*Quercus virginiana*) had the largest average DBH of any canopy species at the park.

6. Yaupon holly (*Ilex vomitoria*) was the most frequently detected seedling species.

7. Wax myrtle (*Morella cerifera*) was the most frequently occurring species in the shrub stratum.

8. Wax myrtle had the highest absolute and relative cover in the shrub stratum.

9. Largeleaf pennywort (*Hydrocotyle bonariensis*) and saltmeadow cordgrass (*Spartina patens*) were the most frequently occurring species in the groundcover stratum.

10. Seaoats (*Uniola paniculata*) had the highest relative cover in the groundcover stratum. Saltmeadow cordgrass had the highest absolute cover in the groundcover stratum, followed very closely by seaoats.

11. The full dataset, and associated metadata, can be acquired from the data store at http://science.nature.nps.gov/nrdata/

Introduction

Overview

Vegetation communities provide many ecosystem services. Among their many functions, they are an important component of food webs and wildlife habitat for many species, and serve as a carbon sink, produce oxygen, cycle nutrients and energy through an ecosystem, influence the local climate, improve water quality, and moderate flooding and erosion. Plant communities also respond to multiple stressors such as changes in air quality, hydrology, disturbance regimes, and climate. Determining trends in vegetation communities is vital to understanding the ecological processes occurring at a site, and identifying stressors and their impacts.

Vegetation communities are dynamic entities with constant changes in composition, cover, distribution, and structure that reflect stressor response, natural or anthropogenic in origin. Disturbance is the primary stressor and regulating mechanism of SECN vegetation communities. The timing, type, and extent of the disturbance generally evoke a distinguishable response in the species composition, diversity, and structure of the landscape (Foster et al. 1998, Turner et al. 1990). The primary natural-disturbance processes in SECN parks are fire and weather (e.g., hurricanes, drought). Anthropogenic influences include fire suppression, landscape fragmentation, altered hydrology, and non-native species introduction.

The SECN is composed of a diverse assemblage of vegetation communities. Approximately 180 vegetation associations (i.e., fine-resolution floristic description), as defined by the National Vegetation and Classification System (FGDC 2008), occur in the SECN. These communities vary widely in distribution, species composition, and structure, and include sparsely vegetated primary dune communities, late successional old-growth bottomland hardwood forest communities, and highly diverse herbaceous-dominated mesic pine savannah communities.

Given the widespread anthropogenic influences in SECN parks and the importance of vegetation communities, quantifying trends in plant cover, frequency, diversity, and distribution is a high priority (DeVivo et al. 2008). Evaluating trends in these metrics provides measures for assessing the ecological integrity and sustainability of southeastern ecosystems, and identifying the need for specific management activities on our park lands. The National Park Service Omnibus Management Act of 1998, and other reinforcing policies and regulations, require park managers "to establish baseline information and to provide information on the long-term trends in the condition of National Park System resources" (Title II, Sec. 204). The vegetation-community monitoring data summarized herein is a tool to assist park managers in fulfilling this mandate.

This report summarizes data collected as a part of the SECN's Vegetation Community Vital Signs monitoring efforts.

Monitoring Objective

- Determine trends in plant species frequency, percent cover, diversity, and distribution in the groundcover, shrub, and canopy strata.

Methods

Study Area

Cape Lookout National Seashore (CALO) is part of the Atlantic coast barrier-island system of the U.S (Figure 1). The 11,430-ha (28,243 ac) Seashore extends approximately 90 km (56 mi) along the east-central coast of North Carolina. The Seashore covers three primary islands: North Core, South Core, and Shackelford Banks from Ocracoke Inlet south to Beaufort Inlet.

Vegetation communities at the Seashore include seaoats dominated dune communities, wax myrtle (*Morella cerifera*) shrub communities, and coastal maritime hammock commonly characterized by Virginia live oak (*Quercus virginiana*). Some small remnant slash pine (*Pinus elliottii*) plantations, planted in the 1970s, occur at the Seashore, however park managers do not plan removal or management of these areas as pine plantations. Except for Shackelford Banks, the bayside of the Seashore consists of salt marsh cordgrass (*Spartina alterniflora* and *S. patens*) communities.

CALO is one of the few barrier islands where natural wind-, tide-, and wave-driven processes of erosion, accretion, and overwash still occur and create a very dynamic environment and vegetation communities. The most significant disturbance regime that affects the Seashore is storm activity (hurricanes and nor'easters). Sea-level rise is also a potential threat. Because the Seashore consists of barrier islands with no road access, the influences of urban development are generally limited. Runoff from mainland sources adds nutrients, fecal coliforms, and contaminants to the waters adjacent to the Seashore. Park managers actively attempt to curb illegal off-trail use by off-road vehicles to prevent the adverse impacts this activity has on barrier island vegetation, dune formation, and natural barrier-island processes. A managed feral horse herd occurs on Shackelford Banks and creates a grazing pressure to which the native plants did not evolve. Several plant species are part of the Seashore's eradication program, including common reed (*Phragmites australis*) (nativity of this species is debated), and two non-native species, Chinese wisteria (*Wisteria sinensis*) and kudzu (*Pueraria lobata*). One federally-threatened species occurs at the Seashore, seabeach amaranth (*Amaranthus pumilus*).

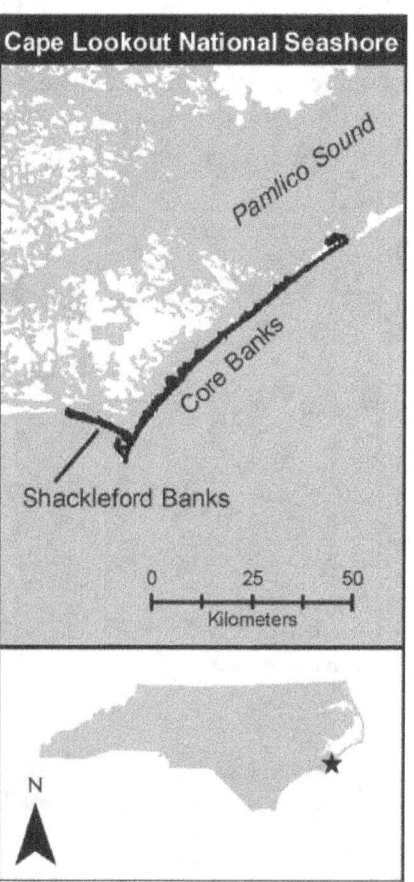

Figure 1. Location of Cape Lookout National Seashore.

CALO has 614 known vascular-plant species, subspecies, and varieties (NPSpecies 2011), including 14 species added to the species list based on these monitoring efforts (Appendix A, Table 2).

Sampling Design

To allow for park-wide inference, the park's administrative boundary was used as the sampling frame, which was divided into a systematic 0.5-ha grid; the center point of each grid cell served as the potential sampling site and the grid cell served as the macroplot. A spatially-balanced sample was drawn from this grid using the Reversed Randomized Quadrant-Recursive Raster (RRQRR) algorithm (Theobald et al. 2007). Alternate points were used when selection criteria (i.e., including safety and access issues) were not met. A sample size of 30 was chosen after consideration of the Seashore's size, hypothesized variability, and logistical issues regarding travel time and conducting monitoring activities in five to six park units per year. Sampling locations are presented in Figure 2. The Seashore was monitored from 7/12/2010 to 8/3/2010.

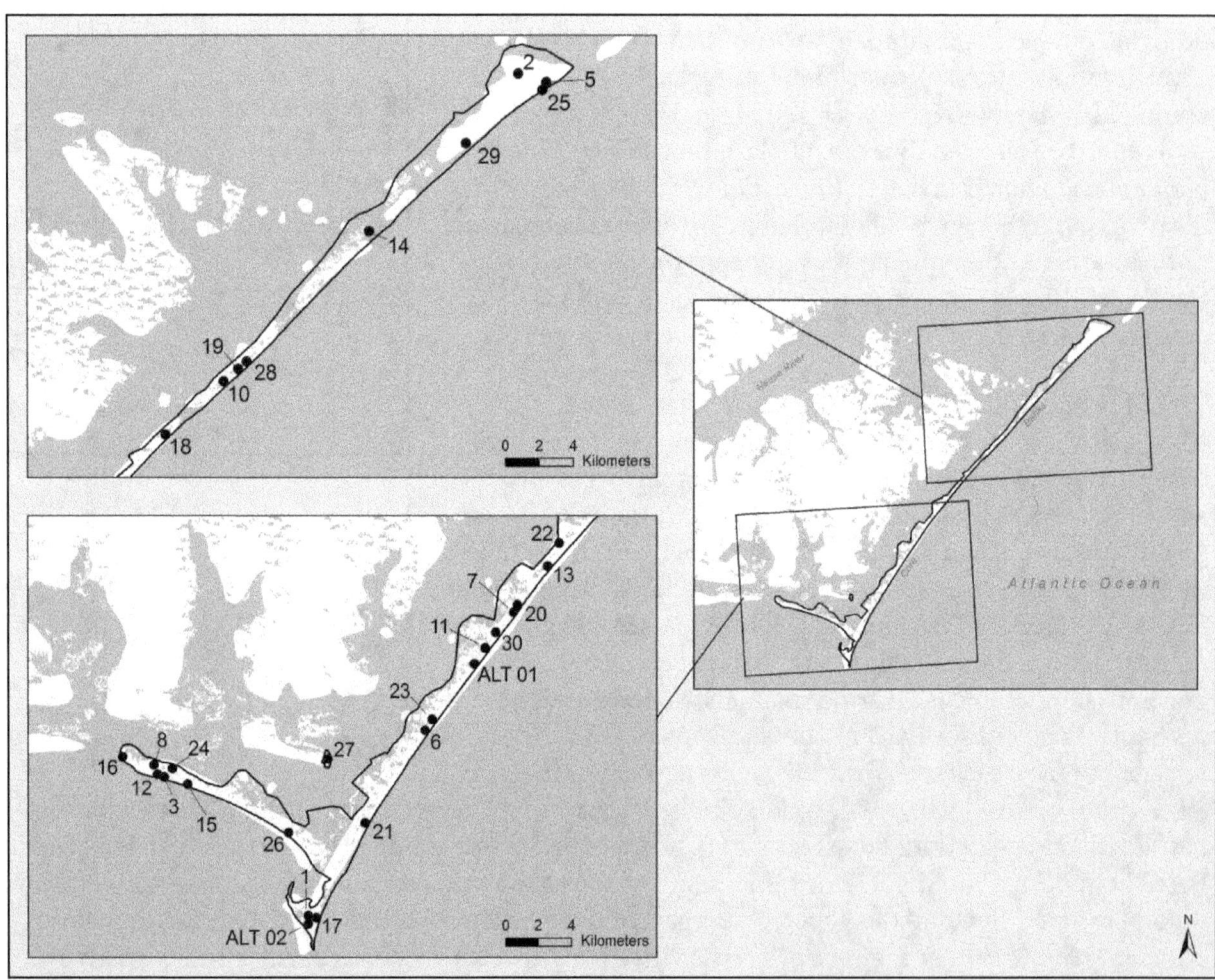

Figure 2. Spatially-balanced random sampling locations at CALO, 2010.

Taxonomic Standards

Species nomenclature for this report follow the current NPSpecies database accessible through the Integration of Resource Management Applications (IRMA) portal (https://irma.nps.gov/App/Portal/Home), which represents the most recent updates from the Integrated Taxonomic Information System (ITIS; http://www.itis.gov). Standards used for the botanical taxonomy in this report and for all work conducted by the Southeast Coast Network are in accordance with those set forth in by ITIS (http://irma.nps.gov/content/help/taxonomy/FAQ.aspx).

Occasionally, if the available characteristics of a plant did not facilitate identification to genus, species, variety, or subspecies, the lowest level of taxonomy identifiable (i.e., the most refined) was used. For example, species of *Dicanthelium* are extremely difficult to identify to species when they lack floral or fruiting structures. In this case, the specimen may only be identified to genus as *Dicanthelium* sp. In the event that a species has more than one variety or subspecies that occurs for a park and the specific variety or subspecies cannot be identified in the field, only the genus and species name were used. For example, several varieties of *Pteridium aquilinum* are known. If for some reason the observer was only able to identify the plant as *Pteridium aquilinum* and not further to variety, only *Pteridium aquilinum* was reported. In these cases, the identified and reported name may not be included in the existing park species list from NPSpecies, only the sub-species or varieties are included in the park species list. Because the genus or species is already known to occur in the park, the general taxonomy will not appear in the "new vascular plant species" (Table 2). In the event a family name, generic name, or genera and species name only (no variety, subspecies, etc.) is used, the most recent taxonomy represented in ITIS is used for these general terms.

Sampling Methodology

Vegetation community measures were divided into three strata based upon diameter at breast height (DBH) of woody species: canopy, shrub, and groundcover. Any non-woody (i.e., herbaceous) species was considered part of the groundcover stratum. Within each stratum, vegetation communities were sampled using a hybrid of methods used by the North Carolina Vegetation Survey nested-subplot design (Peet et al. 1998) within a circular plot similar to the Forest Inventory and Analysis protocol (Bechtold and Patterson 2005).

Plot Layout

The layout consisted of a circular plot with a radius of 15 m within the 0.5-ha macroplot. Subplots were systematically placed along six transects that radiated out from the center point at azimuths of 0°/360°, 60°, 120°, 180°, 240°, and 300° (Figure 3). To avoid overlap, subplots originated four meters from the macroplot (i.e., 0.5-ha grid) center point and extended away from the center point. Five measures were collected in the nested subplots within each plot: canopy cover, shrub cover, DBH, canopy-species seedling frequency, and herbaceous cover. Canopy cover was measured from the center point of the 0.5-ha macroplot. Shrub coverage was measured in two 2 × 4 m shrub plots along each transect. The shrub plots were further subdivided into 2 × 2 m subplots to improve cover-estimation accuracy and precision because cover-estimation error increases with plot size (solid gray shading, Figure 3). Groundcover coverage, groundcover nested frequency, and seedling frequency was measured in two 1 × 1 m groundcover plots (solid black shading, Figure 3) along each transect. Canopy species DBH was measured in three sections, each representing 1/3 of the total circular plot (hashed gray shading,

Figure 3). A comprehensive species list was also compiled for all species occurring in the 0.5-ha macroplot. This macroplot list supplemented the list of species detected within the vegetation-community sampling plot (i.e., in the canopy, shrub, and groundcover plots).

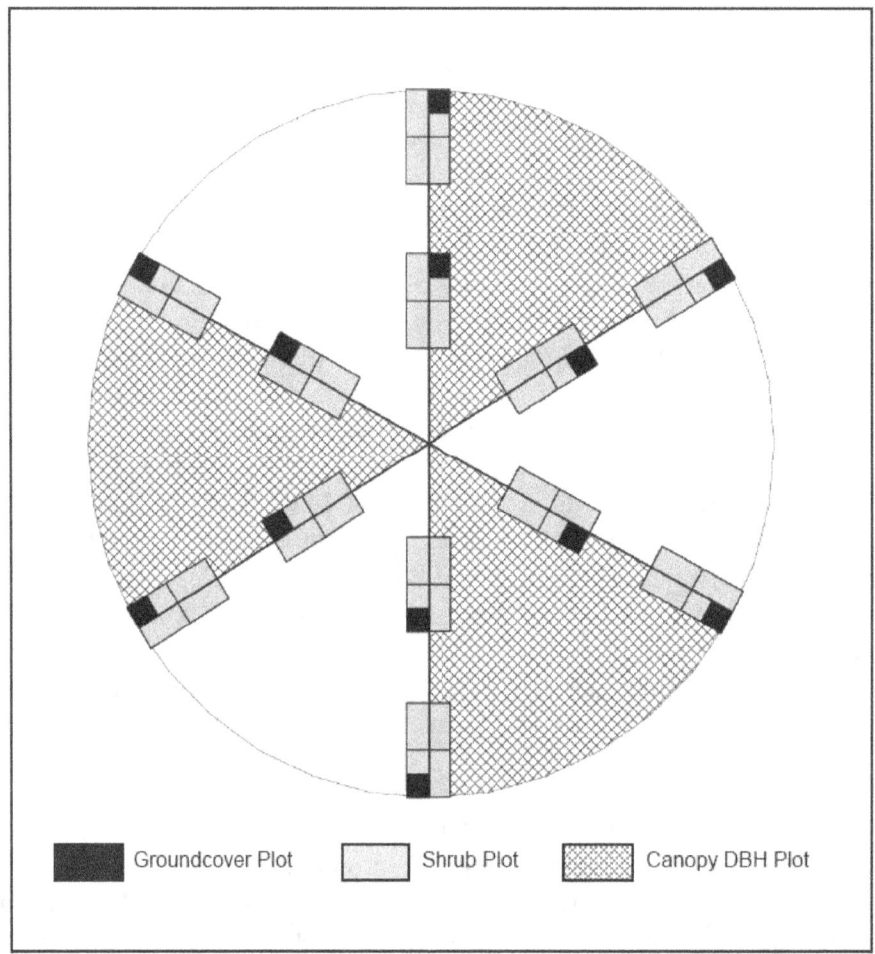

Figure 3. Southeast Coast Network vegetation-community monitoring plot layout.

Canopy Measures
Absolute canopy cover was estimated in the four cardinal directions with a concave spherical densiometer placed on a 1.1-m tall tripod at the plot center. Canopy cover reported is the mean of three observers across the four cardinal directions. The circular plot was subdivided into six sections occurring between the 0–60°, 120–180°, and 240–300° compass transects of the circular plot. Diameter at breast height (i.e., 1.37 m above the ground) was measured to the nearest millimeter for all trees (identified by species) with a diameter greater than or equal to 4 cm that occur within the 0–60°, 120–180°, and 240–300° section.

Shrub Measures
Shrub cover of all shrub species was visually estimated for each of the twelve 2 × 4 m plots. A common source of error in visual estimation of vegetation cover is that as plot size increases, cover-estimation error increases. Each shrub plot was therefore sub-divided into two 2 × 2 m subplots. The plots are situated at 15 m and 8 m (extending toward the plot center) along each of the transect lines of the circular plot. Shrub cover was categorized into one of seven coverage

classes (Table 1) for each subplot. A coverage class of zero (Table 1) is assumed for any shrub species not detected and not recorded on the datasheet. The measurements of subplots were combined by averaging the midpoint for the coverage class in the two shrub subplots resulting in a total shrub cover estimate for the 2 × 4 m plot. The authors have established consistent performance in the accuracy and precision of visual-cover estimates within and across observers in plots this size.

Groundcover Measures

Groundcover was visually estimated in each of the twelve 1 × 1 m plots situated on the clockwise side at 15 m and 8 m (extending toward the plot center) along each of the transect lines of the circular plot. Groundcover was categorized into one of seven coverage classes (Table 1) for each plot. A coverage class of zero (Table 1) is assumed for any groundcover species not detected and not recorded on the datasheet. The authors have established through trials that these coverage classes are discriminatory and repeatable across observers. Canopy-species seedling counts were estimated by counting the number of seedlings that occur in each of the 1 × 1 m plots.

Table 1. Cover estimation coverage class, percent cover range, and value used for analyses.

Coverage Class	Percent Cover Range	Value Used for Analyses
0	0%	0.0
1	Trace (<1%)	0.5
2	1-5%	2.5
3	5-25%	15.0
4	25-50%	37.5
5	50-75%	62.5
6	75-95%	85.0
7	95-100%	97.5

Data Analysis

Because this is the first year of this protocol's implementation at the Seashore, only the status of the elements presented in the aforementioned monitoring objective are determined, except diversity and distribution. The data in this report are presented by plot and pooled across plots. Sampling locations are presented in Figure 2 and summaries by plot are presented in Tables 3-9.

The summaries in this report include (a) new species detected (Table 2), (b) canopy cover (Table 3), (c) canopy species size (Table 4), (d) seedling frequency (Table 5), (e) shrub species relative cover and frequency (Table 6), shrub species absolute cover and frequency (Table 7), (f) groundcover relative cover and frequency (Table 8), (g) groundcover absolute cover and frequency (Table 9), (h) species detected (Appendix A), and (i) species composition within and across macroplots (Appendix B).

Findings

We detected 135 species, subspecies, and varieties during this monitoring effort (Appendix A), including 14 new species, subspecies, or varieties not previously known to occur at the Seashore (Table 2).

Table 2. New plant species, sub-species, or varieties found at Cape Lookout National Seashore, 2010, and recommended NPSpecies classifications.

Species	Abundance	Nativity	Pest	Management Priority	Exploitation Concerns
Andropogon glomeratus var. glomeratus	Unknown	Native	No	No	No
Campsis radicans	Unknown	Native	No	No	No
Centrosema virginianum	Unknown	Native	No	No	No
Fraxinus caroliniana	Unknown	Native	No	No	No
Galium tinctorium	Unknown	Native	No	No	No
Gaylussacia dumosa	Unknown	Native	No	No	No
Magnolia grandiflora	Unknown	Native	No	No	No
Phragmites australis	Unknown	Native[a]	Unknown	Yes	No
Polystichum acrostichoides	Unknown	Native	No	No	No
Potentilla canadensis	Unknown	Native	No	No	No
Rosa multiflora	Unknown	Non-native	No	Possibly	No
Rubus cuneifolius	Unknown	Native	No	No	No
Sabatia calycina	Unknown	Native	No	No	No
Sabatia campanulata	Unknown	Native	No	No	No

[a] Nativity is debated. This species is categorized as a native species on the PLANTS database (http://plants.usda.gov/java/) but is considered a nuisance is some states, including North Carolina (http://www.invasiveplantatlas.org/whereinvasive.html?sub=3062).

Measures of Community Structure

Canopy cover was variable across the all sampling locations at the park ($\bar{x}$ = 10.85%, SD = 25.56; Table 3). Virginia live oak had the largest average DBH of any tree at the park ($\bar{x}$ = 20.49 cm, SD = 10.18), however Virginia live oak only occurred in two sampling locations (Table 4). The most frequently detected seedling was yaupon holly (*Ilex vomitoria*) (0.81/m^2; Table 5). Wax myrtle was the most frequently occurring shrub species at the park (f = 94.12) and had the highest relative cover of all other shrub species ($\bar{x}$ = 50.11%, SD = 31.73; Table 6). Wax myrtle also had the highest absolute cover in the shrub stratum at the park ($\bar{x}$ = 21.07%, SD = 19.02; Table 7). Largeleaf pennywort (*Hydrocotyle bonariensis*) and saltmeadow cordgrass (*Spartina patens*) were the most frequently occurring species (83.33 and 73.33%, respectively) in the groundcover stratum (Table 8). Seaoats had the highest relative cover in the groundcover stratum ($\bar{x}$ = 9.05%, SD = 11.71), followed by saltmeadow cordgrass ($\bar{x}$ = 7.79%, SD = 9.26; Table 8). Saltmeadow cordgrass had the highest absolute cover in the groundcover stratum ($\bar{x}$ = 46.43%, SD = 19.36), followed closely by seaoats ($\bar{x}$ = 16.42%, SD = 21.45; Table 9).

Table 3. Average canopy cover in vegetation monitoring sampling locations at Cape Lookout National Seashore, 2010.

Sampling Location	Average Canopy Cover	Standard Deviation
1	81.25	5.63
2	0	0
3	0	0
5	0	0
6	0	0
7	0	0
8	0	0
10	0.17	0.29
11	0	0
12	0	0
13	0	0
14	0	0
15	0	0
16	0	0
17	22.00	3.38
18	0	0
19	0	0
20	0	0
21	0	0
22	0.75	0.43
23	15.83	3
24	84.67	2.84
25	0	0
26	0	0
27	78.67	3.33
28	0	0
29	0	0
30	0	0
A1	0	0
A2	42.17	0.38
Park-wide Average	**10.85**	**25.56**

Table 4. Average canopy species size, measured as diameter (cm) at breast height (DBH) for species sampled in vegetation monitoring sampling locations at Cape Lookout National Seashore, 2010. Numbers in parentheses indicate the number of individual trees measured within each plot.

Scientific Name	Average	Standard Deviation	1	2	3	5	6	7	8	10	11	12	13	14	15	16	17
Baccharis halimifolia	5.38	0.74															5.54 (5)
Fraxinus sp.	4.90									4.90 (1)							
Ilex opaca	8.56	3.86															
Ilex vomitoria	5.44	1.37								5.62 (15)				6.20 (4)			7.94 (5)
Juniperus virginiana	10.73	8.77		12.80 (1)						5.70 (1)							
Morella cerifera	5.06	1.37								4.47 (3)				4.10 (2)			4.90 (4)
Osmanthus americanus	5.70																
Persea borbonia	6.36	2.71															
Pinus taeda	19.54	9.77															18.01 (7)
Quercus laurifolia	10.51	3.68															
Quercus virginiana	20.49	10.18															
Dead																	
Juniperus virginiana	8.50	6.09															
Morella cerifera	6.80	2.05								5.80 (3)							
Pinus taeda	6.00																
Quercus laurifolia	6.65	2.76															
Quercus virginiana	7.50																
Unidentified																	
Tracheobionta	7.90	2.97															

Table 4. Continued (sampling locations 18–A2).

Scientific Name	Average	Standard Deviation	18	19	20	21	22	23	24	25	26	27	28	29	30	A1	A2
Bacchanis halimifolia	5.38	0.74					5.10 (3)										
Fraxinus sp.	4.90																
Ilex opaca	8.56	3.86										9.56 (8)					
Ilex vomitoria	5.44	1.37				4.20 (1)			4.15 (2)								4.33 (4)
Juniperus virginiana	10.73	8.77				6.10 (5)	7.30 (7)	6.35 (4)	24.40 (9)								8.43 (18)
Morella cerifera	5.06	1.37				4.75 (2)	4.10 (1)		5.41 (8)								6.60 (2)
Osmanthus americanus	5.70											5.70 (1)					
Persea borbonia	6.36	2.71				6.20 (4)						7.00 (1)					
Pinus taeda	19.54	9.77										20.36 (13)					
Quercus laurifolia	10.51	3.68										10.51 (19)					
Quercus virginiana	20.49	10.18							28.01 (7)			15.71 (11)					
Dead																	
Juniperus virginiana	8.50	6.09					5.60 (2)		9.95 (4)								
Morella cerifera	6.80	2.05										9.80 (1)					
Pinus taeda	6.00											6.00 (1)					
Quercus laurifolia	6.65	2.76										6.65 (2)					
Quercus virginiana	7.50											7.50 (1)					
Unidentified																	
Tracheobionta	7.90	2.97							7.90 (2)								

Table 5. Seedling frequency for canopy and shrub species in vegetation monitoring sampling locations at Cape Lookout National Seashore, 2010.

Species	Total Seedlings	Seedlings/m2	Std Dev	Sampling Location														
				1	2	3	5	6	7	8	10	11	12	13	14	15	16	17
Baccharis halimifolia	37	0.10	0.56															
Bomchia frutescens	12	0.03	0.12												0.08			
Callicarpa americana	2	0.01	0.03															
Cynanchum angustifolium	3	0.01	0.05															
Gaylussacia dumosa	30	0.08	0.46															
Ilex opaca	14	0.04	0.21															
Ilex vomitoria	291	0.81	3.13								16.42				0.33			
Juniperus virginiana	24	0.07	0.37															
Morella cerifera	92	0.26	0.5		0.25			1.25			0.25				2.25			0.42
Osmanthus americanus	8	0.02	0.1															
Persea borbonia	1	0	0.02															0.08
Pinus taeda	1	0	0.02															
Quercus virginiana	88	0.24	0.98															
Vaccinium stamineum	2	0.01	0.03															

Table 5. Continued (sampling locations 18–A2).

Species	Total Seedlings	Seedlings/m2	Std Dev	Sampling Location														
				18	19	20	21	22	23	24	25	26	27	28	29	30	A1	A2
Baccharis halimifolia	37	0.10	0.56															
Bomchia frutescens	12	0.03	0.12												0.42			
Callicarpa americana	2	0.01	0.03							0.17								
Cynanchum angustifolium	3	0.01	0.05															
Gaylussacia dumosa	30	0.08	0.46										2.50			0.25		
Ilex opaca	14	0.04	0.21							1.17								
Ilex vomitoria	291	0.81	3.13				0.83	0.92		5.75					3.08			
Juniperus virginiana	24	0.07	0.37							2.00								
Morella cerifera	92	0.26	0.5		1.08		0.33	0.50			0.25		0.17		0.33	0.33		
Osmanthus americanus	8	0.02	0.1							0.17			0.50					
Persea borbonia	1	0	0.02										0.08					
Pinus taeda	1	0	0.02															
Quercus virginiana	88	0.24	0.98							2.50			4.83					0.75
Vaccinium stamineum	2	0.01	0.03										0.17					

Table 6. Percent of vegetation cover (relative cover) and frequency of occurrence of shrub species in vegetation monitoring sampling locations at Cape Lookout National Seashore, 2010.

Species	Frequency	Average	Std Dev	1*	2	3	4	5	6	7	8	9	10	11	12	13	14	15	16	17
Baccharis angustifolia	16.67	2.82	9.97					7.22					4.22							
Baccharis halimifolia	33.33	3.34	6.60		15.46			10.31	10.75								1.94			8.75
Borrichia frutescens	16.67	2.06	5.70										5.91				27.23			
Callicarpa americana	3.33	0.38	2.11																	
Gaylussacia dumosa	3.33	0.65	3.58																	
Ilex glabra	3.33	0.24	1.29																	
Ilex opaca	6.67	1.52	6.78																	
Ilex vomitoria	33.33	5.75	11.09	P					4.24				32.69				32.34			
Iva frutescens	23.33	2.81	6.69					6.19					1.45				4.2			
Juniperus virginiana	20.00	0.35	0.84	P													1.94			1.33
Kosteletzkya virginica	3.33	0.03	0.16																	
Morella cerifera	56.67	28.61	34.13	P	84.54			76.29	85.01				55.73				32.34			73.76
Osmanthus americanus	6.67	0.59	2.30																	
Persea borbonia	16.67	0.48	1.49	P																6.08
Pinus taeda	3.33	0.34	1.84																	10.08
Quercus laurifolia	3.33	0.43	2.34																	
Quercus virginiana	6.67	0.54	2.13	P																
Rosa multiflora	3.33	N/A	N/A																	
Vaccinium arboreum	3.33	0.01	0.05																	
Vaccinium staminum	3.33	0.01	0.05																	

* Species identified with a "P" at Sampling Location 1 were identified as present, but due to logistical issues at this location, further measurements were unable to be collected.

Table 6. Continued (sampling locations 18–A2).

Species	Frequency	Average	Std Dev	18	19	20	21	22	23	24	25	26	27	28	29	30	A1	A2
										Sampling Location								
Baccharis angustifolia	16.67	2.82	9.97		21.51													
Baccharis halimifolia	33.33	3.34	6.60				4.61	5.47	28.88						13.02	50.87		0.86
Borrichia frutescens	16.67	2.05	5.70					11.74							5.58	11.03		
Callicarpa americana	3.33	0.38	2.11							11.54								
Gaylussacia dumosa	3.33	0.65	3.58										19.62					
Ilex glabra	3.33	0.24	1.29										7.08					
Ilex opaca	6.67	1.52	6.78							36.26			9.26					
Ilex vomitoria	33.33	5.75	11.09				25.3	31.99	14.37	19.08						0.66		6.15
Iva frutescens	23.33	2.81	6.69					22.03	7.4						23.72	19.32		
Juniperus virginiana	20.00	0.35	0.84					3.38					1.63					2
Kosteletzkya virginica	3.33	0.03	0.16							0.89								
Morella cerifera	56.67	28.61	34.13		78.49		63.84	25.4	49.36	19.37	100		26.43		57.67	18.12		90.13
Osmanthus americanus	6.67	0.59	2.30							6.65			10.9					
Persea borbonia	16.67	0.48	1.49				5.36						1.63					0.86
Pinus taeda	3.33	0.34	1.84															
Quercus laurifolia	3.33	0.43	2.34										12.81					
Quercus virginiana	6.67	0.54	2.13							6.21			10.08					
Rosa multiflora	3.33	N/A	N/A															
Vaccinium arboreum	3.33	0.01	0.05										0.27					
Vaccinium stamineum	3.33	0.01	0.05										0.27					

16

Table 7. Percent area covered (absolute cover) and frequency of occurrence of shrub species sampled in vegetation monitoring sampling locations at Cape Lookout National Seashore, 2010.

Species	Frequency	Average	Std Dev	Sampling Location														
				1*	2	3	5	6	7	8	10	11	14	15	16	17	19	21
Baccharis angustifolia	16.67	2.37	9.71				0.73				3.65						5.63	0.63
Baccharis halimifolia	33.33	1.71	4.30		3.13		1.04	1.58					0.63			4.79		3.23
Borrichia frutescens	16.67	1.33	3.09								5.1		8.77					
Callicarpa americana	3.33	0.33	1.63															
Gaylussacia dumosa	3.33	0.30	1.50															
Ilex glabra	3.33	0.11	0.54															
Ilex opaca	6.67	1.16	5.13															
Ilex vomitoria	33.33	4.45	8.04	P				0.63			28.23		10.42					17.71
Iva frutescens	23.33	1.94	4.73				0.63				1.25		1.35					
Juniperus virginiana	20.00	0.24	0.55	P									0.63			0.73		
Kosteletzkya virginica	3.33	0.03	0.13	P														
Morella cerifera	56.67	12.04	14.03	P	17.08		7.71	12.52			48.13		10.42			40.42	20.52	44.69
Osmanthus americanus	6.67	0.35	1.23															
Persea borbonia	16.67	0.35	1.00	P												3.33		3.75
Pinus taeda	3.33	0.22	1.10													5.52		
Quercus laurifolia	3.33	0.20	0.98															
Quercus virginiana	6.67	0.33	1.14															
Rosa multiflora	3.33			P														
Vaccinium arboreum	3.33	0.00	0.02															
Vaccinium stamineum	3.33	0.00	0.02															

* Species identified with a "P" at Sampling Location 1 were identified as present, but due to logistical issues at this location, further measurements were unable to be collected.

Table 7. Continued (sampling locations 22–A2).

Species	Frequency	Average	Std Dev					Sampling Location					
				22	23	24	25	26	27	29	30	A1	A2
Baccharis angustifolia	16.67	2.37	9.71								48.54		
Baccharis halimifolia	33.33	1.71	4.30	3.54	21.15					2.92			0.63
Borrichia frutescens	16.67	1.33	3.09	7.6						1.25	10.52		
Callicarpa americana	3.33	0.33	1.63			8.13							
Gaylussacia dumosa	3.33	0.30	1.50						7 5				
Ilex glabra	3.33	0.11	0.54						2.71				
Ilex opaca	6.67	1.16	5.13			25.54			3.54				
Ilex vomitoria	33.33	4.45	8.04	20.73	10.52	13.44					0.63		4.48
Iva frutescens	23.33	1.94	4.73	14.27	5.42					5.31	18.44		
Juniperus virginiana	20.00	0.24	0.55	2.19					0.63				1.46
Kosteletzkya virginica	3.33	0.03	0.13			0.63							
Morella cerifera	56.67	12.04	14.03	16.46	36.15	13.65	1.56		10.1	12.92	17.29		65.63
Osmanthus americanus	6.67	0.35	1.23			4.69			4.17				
Persea borbonia	16.67	0.35	1.00						0.63				0.63
Pinus taeda	3.33	0.22	1.10										
Quercus laurifolia	3.33	0.20	0.98						4.9				
Quercus virginiana	6.67	0.33	1.14			4.38			3.85				
Rosa multiflora	3.33	N/A	N/A										
Vaccinium arboreum	3.33	0.00	0.02						0.1				
Vaccinium stamineum	3.33	0.00	0.02						0.1				

Table 8. Percent of vegetation cover (relative cover) and frequency of occurrence of groundcover species in vegetation monitoring sampling locations at Cape Lookout National Seashore, 2010.

Species	Frequency	Avg	Std Dev	Sampling Point																													
				1*	2	3	5	6	7	8	10	11	12	13	14	15	16	17	18	19	20	21	22	23	24	25	26	27	28	29	30	A1	A2
Ambrosia artemisiifolia	6.67	0.06	0.25					1.27				0.58																						
Ampelopsis arborea	10	0.37	1.61																					8.74	1.14						1.36		
Andropogon glomeratus var. glomeratus	20	0.32	0.95		1.12		4.55				0.64									0.65						2.57					0.1		
Baccharis halimifolia	3.33	0.07	0.38																											2.06			
Berchemia scandens	6.67	0.08	0.32																			1.26			1.24								
Boehmeria cylindrica	3.33	0.05	0.26																						1.43								
Borrichia frutescens	10	0.05	0.17												0.1								0.62							0.72			
Calicarpa americana	3.33	0.01	0.03																						0.19								
Cenchrus sp.	3.33	0.04	0.19																1.06														
Centella asiatica	6.67	0.05	0.2															0.9							0.67								
Chamaesyce polygonifolia	40	0.17	0.54		0.09	0.12			0.23	0.23				0.02			0.49		2.93	0.65	0.02						0.11		0.12			0.03	
Chasmanthium laxum	3.33	0.04	0.23																						1.24								
Cirsium sp.	3.33	0.01	0.08																			0.42											
Cladium jamaicense	6.67	0.08	0.36				0.5				1.91																						
Commelina erecta	36.67	0.35	0.78			0.35		3.09	0.81			0.78	0.13			0.79		0.13			0.11	0.42								2.88				1.05
Conyza canadensis	53.33	0.95	1.6		0.66	4.99		0.11	2.08	0.13			3.7	0.57		6.13	2.36		2.13	0.86	0.34					0.15			2.24	0.1		1.87	
Croton punctatus	13.33	0.06	0.2			0.35							0.02						8									0.76						
Cynanchum angustifolium	43.33	0.9	1.71				2.07	4.48			1.38	0.58			0.1			2.38		0.75		0.84		1.24	2.58						1.23	8.02		1.32
Cyperus sp.	3.33	0.02	0.12		0.66																													
Desmodium sp.	3.33	0.01	0.03																						0.19								
Dichanthelium sp.	6.67	0.03	0.12					0.27			0.64																							
Diodia teres	10	0.04	0.13							0.43		0.58					0.12																	
Diodia virginiana	6.67	0.08	0.36															1.88							0.67								
Eleocharis sp.	6.67	0.14	0.66								3.61														0.57								
Elephantopus sp.	3.33	0.03	0.16																						0.86								
Elymus virginicus	10	0.1	0.43								0.74												2.28	0.07									
Eremochloa ophiuroides	6.67	0.15	0.83													0.1													4.54				

19

Table 8. Continued.

Species	Frequency	Avg	Std Dev	1*	2	3	5	6	7	8	10	11	12	13	14	15	16	17	18	19	20	21	22	23	24	25	26	27	28	29	30	A1	A2
Eustachys petraea	10	0.08	0.32						0.75				0.11																				
Fimbristylis sp.	10	0.45	1.75				9.09																			3.21				1.61	1.23			
Gaillardia pulchella	10	0.24	1.07					5.83																						0.69				
Galium obtusum	3.33	0.03	0.16									0.58													0.88								
Gaylussacia dumosa	3.33	0.15	0.8																									4.4					
Heterotheca subaxillaris	46.67	1.46	2.02		0.09	0.92		2.91	2.54	2.25		4.27		4.66		1.88	6.15	0.75			5.62						3.92		4.4			3.34	
Hydrocotyle bonariensis	83.33	3.94	3.73		6.75	0.95	12.07	3.11	4.5	4.16	1.91	10.38	1.38	7.84		1.48	4.26	6.51	0.8	8.5	6.54	6.76			0.43	0.67	11.57		3.34	8.33		3.23	0.61
Ilex opaca	3.33	0.07	0.37																						2								
Ilex vomitoria	16.67	0.49	1.68								8.28				0.59								0.42	1.24		4.28							
Ipomoea sagittata	20	0.39	1.43								1.29												0.42	0.62	7.74	1.14					0.62			
Ipomoea sp.	3.33	N/A	N/A	P																													
Juncus canadensis	13.33	0.29	0.98		1.22		2.48																			4.75				0.21			
Juncus roemerianus	40	4.48	8.01		12.46		1.49				11.36				24.46			5.76		1.29		10.95	26.06	11.25						0.1	24.36		5
Juncus sp.	6.67	0.02	0.1					0.55																	0.13							
Juniperus virginiana	3.33	0.03	0.17																						0.91								
Lactuca canadensis	3.33	0	0.02		0.09																												
Lythrum lineare	6.67	0.05	0.21																			0.42										1.09		
Melothria pendula	3.33	0.02	0.12							0.64																							
Mikania scandens	26.67	0.64	1.42		5.34		2.64				4.56				3.27							0.49		1.79	0.57					0.64			
Mitchella repens	3.33	0.15	0.8																						4.38							
Morella cerifera	40	0.43	0.72		0.56			2.73			1.27				2.08			1.5		1.4		1.05				0.9		0.05		0.21		0.53
Muhlenbergia capillaris	3.33	0.12	0.65																										3.57			
Oenothera humifusa	60	1.34	1.39		0.09	4.16		2.37	3.02	2.63		0.58	3.45	2.78		3.56	2.62		1.89	0.75	2.06				1.67	2.4		2.33	0.82		2.86	
Opuntia humifusa	3.33	0.05	0.27																										1.5			
Opuntia sp.	13.33	0.13	0.49			2.66							0.45			0.3						0.42										
Osmanthus americanus	6.67	0.02	0.06																						0.19			0.29				
Oxypolis sp.	3.33	0	0.02		0.09																											
Panicum amarum	23.33	0.96	2.68						1.41	0.08		1.86		11.93			0.71			0.65	9.06											
Panicum sp.	6.67	0.09	0.4																						2.11				0.69			
Parthenocissus quinquefolia	23.33	1.01	2.66	P						3.4								1					4.81		7.81	1.52							11.67

20

Table 8. Continued.

Species	Frequency	Avg	Std Dev	1*	2	3	5	6	7	8	10	11	12	13	14	15	16	17	18	19	20	21	22	23	24	25	26	27	28	29	30	A1	A2
Paspalum vaginatum	10	0.2	0.87				0.5																4.76								0.62			
Passiflora lutea	3.33	0.01	0.03																						0.19									
Persea borbonia	3.33	0	0.02															0.13															
Phyla nodiflora	16.67	0.14	0.41		0.02															1.29		0.49		1.79	0.67								
Physalis viscosa	40	0.26	0.46			0.23		0.55	0.69			1.75	0.04	0.11			0.71			0.65	1.38	0.98						0.04	0.81					
Pinus taeda	3.33	0	0.02																										0.13					
Polygonum sp.	6.67	0.08	0.34		1.78																		0.57										
Polystichum acrostichoides	3.33	0.02	0.1																					0.57										
Potentilla canadensis	3.33	0.03	0.14																					0.78										
Pteridium aquilinum	3.33	0.4	2.17																								11.88							
Quercus virginiana	6.67	0.22	0.86																					3.05					3.68					
Rhynchospora colorata	10	0.04	0.14																	0.11		0.42		0.67									
Rhynchospora sp.	6.67	0.03	0.14																					0.19	0.77								
Rubus cuneifolius	6.67	0.16	0.63		3.09													1.63															
Rubus sp.	3.33	0.02	0.1																														
Rubus trivialis	26.67	0.28	0.65	P				1.64			0.85				0.1			0.75			2.93	1.24			0.57							0.79
Sanicula canadensis	3.33	0.02	0.12																					0.67									
Schizachyrium scoparium var litorale	13.33	0.08	0.22					0.73										0.75			0.42											0.53
Schoenoplectus americanus	13.33	0.16	0.53		2.62					1.27												0.42			0.57								
Setaria parviflora	3.33	0	0.02																	0.11													
Smilax sp.	26.67	1.24	2.77	P																			7.34	2.79	8.38			7.07			1.91		9.12
Solidago sempervirens	36.67	0.79	1.59				6.2	1.82	0.69		0.87	0.58								0.65		0.42					4.75			2.07	4.42	1.09	0.8	
Solidago sp.	13.33	0.16	0.61					0.55													3.28								0.8					0.09
Spartina patens	73.33	7.79	9.26		13.02		19.83	12.83	4.52		4.25	19.39		2.65	22.57			2.63	3.19	29.92	16.17	7.11	4.03	8.17				6.68	32.92	5.91	0.13	2.89
Spiranthes sp.	3.33	0	0.02				0.08																											
Strophostyles helvola	13.33	0.15	0.55														2.47													0.14			1.79	
Thelypteris sp.	3.33	0.11	0.59																					3.24									
Toxicodendron radicans	33.33	2.95	5.83	P	3						2.02							12.53				16.67	1.86	12.89	8						9.63		21.75
Typha sp.	3.33	0.02	0.1		0.56																												
Uniola paniculata	50	9.05	11.71		27.61		2.28	22.96		23.4	5.14		27.75	17.23		30.27	18.14		22.9	1.29	7.34					30.29		8.76			26.06	

21

Table 8. Continued.

Species	Frequency	Avg	Std Dev	1	2	3	5	6	7	8	10	11	12	13	14	15	16	17	18	19	20	21	22	23	24	25	26	27	28	29	30	A1	A2
																												Sampling Point					
Vaccinium stamineum	3.33	0.03	0.15																									0.8					
Vitis rotundifolia	10	0.23	0.81																						0.57			2.8					3.51
Unidentified																																	
Asteraceae	10	0.18	0.68										3.12												0.1			2.14					
Cyperaceae	13.33	0.08	0.34								0.11														0.43						0.1			
Fabaceae	10	0.03	0.11					0.09	0.12																0.57								
Lamiaceae	3.33	0.04	0.2					1.09																									
Magnoliopsida	10	0.07	0.25					1.27																	0.19								
Poaceae	30	0.4	1		1.69	0.14									1.19	0.59		0.75		0.65					0.57	4.88			2.07		0.18		
Ground Condition																																	
Bare ground	76.67	16.5	16.7		5.53	39.74		2	27.69	41.93	1.59	16.68	28.86	21.86		30.27	44.77	3.13	45.79	14.21	21.21				0.76	34.18	36.39	0.8	30.3	10.39	36	34	0.53
Exposed humus	20	0.8	2.28				1.07				0.64				0.2							5.58	8.27					8.27					
Leaf litter or duff	96.67	31.52	12.61	39.45	17.79	37.44	19.3	28.75	24.03	47.65	35.2	30.98	30.15	45.35	24.63	17.2	56.88	18.5	35.63	30.15	32.64	40.43	33.52	40.37	17.73	22.01	60.6	22.35	35.18	37.63	23.54	40.6	1
Upland non-vascular plants or lichens	10	1.09	5.33					29.13																	0.1				3.46				

* Species identified with a "P" at Sampling Location 1 were identified as present, but due to logistical issues at this location, further measurements were unable to be collected.

Table 9. Percent area covered (absolute cover) and frequency of occurrence by groundcover species sampled in vegetation monitoring sampling locations at Cape Lookout National Seashore, 2010.

Species	Frequency	Avg	Std Dev	1*	2	3	5	6	7	8	10	11	12	13	14	15	16	17	18	19	20	21	22	23	24	25	26	27	28	29	30	A1	A2
																		Sampling Location															
Ambrosia artemisiifolia	6.67	0.14	0.57					2.92																								
Ampelopsis arborea	10	1.03	4.66																					25.42	2.5					3.13		
Andropogon glomeratus var. glomeratus	20	0.69	2.23			2.5	11.46				1.25									1.25						4.17			0.21			
Baccharis halimifolia	3.33	0.14	0.76																											4.17			
Berchemia scandens	6.67	0.22	0.83																			3.75			2.71							
Borrichia cylindrica	3.33	0.1	0.57																						3.13							
Borrichia frutescens	10	0.1	0.34																				1.25						1.46			
Callicarpa americana	3.33	0.01	0.08												0.21										0.42							
Cenchrus sp.	3.33	0.06	0.3																1.67													
Centella asiatica	6.67	0.1	0.38															1.5									1.46					
Chamaesyce polygonifolia	40	0.28	0.86		0.21	0.21			0.42	0.38				0.04			0.88		4.58	1.25	0.04						0.21		0.21			0.04	
Chasmanthium laxum	3.33	0.09	0.49																						2.71							
Cirsium sp.	3.33	0.04	0.23																			1.25										
Cladium jamaicense	6.67	0.17	0.71				1.25				3.75																					
Commelina erecta	36.67	0.74	1.63			0.63		7.08	1.46			1.67	0.25			1.67		0.21			0.21	1.25										
Conyza canadensis	53.33	1.76	3.09		1.46	9		0.25	3.75	0.21			6.92	1.08		12.92	4.17		3.33	1.67	0.63					0.25		4.04	0.21			2.92	
Croton punctatus	13.33	0.11	0.36			0.63							0.04																				
Cynanchum angustifolium	43.33	2.05	3.96				5.21								0.21			3.96		1.46		2.5	2.5	7.5						2.5	18.38		3.13
Cyperus sp.	3.33	0.05	0.27		1.46																												
Desmodium sp.	3.33	0.01	0.08																						0.42							
Dichanthelium sp.	6.67	0.06	0.25					0.63																								
Diodia teres	10	0.07	0.26							0.71		1.25																				
Diodia virginiana	6.67	0.15	0.62														0.21	3.13							1.46							
Eleocharis sp.	6.67	0.28	1.31								7.08														1.25							
Elephantopus sp.	3.33	0.06	0.34																						1.88							
Elymus virginicus	10	0.21	0.87								1.46												4.58	0.21								
Eremochloa ophuroides	6.67	0.24	1.29													0.21												7.08					
Eustachys petraea	10	0.15	0.57							1.25			0.21																2.92				
Fimbristylis sp.	10	1.02	4.26				22.92	13.33																						2.5			
Gaillardia pulchella	10	0.53	2.44									1.25														5.21				1.25			
Galium obtusum	3.33	0.06	0.35																						1.92							
Gaylussacia dumosa	3.33	0.23	1.26																									6.88					
Heterotheca subaxillaris	46.67	2.74	3.77		0.21	1.67		6.67	4.58	3.75		9.17		9.17		3.96	10.88	1.25		16.46	10.21						7.5		7.96			5.21	
Hydrocotyle bonariensis	83.33	7.96	8.05	15	1.71	30.42		7.13	8.13	6.92	3.75	22.29	2.58	14.79		3.13	7.54	10.83	1.25	16.46	11.88	20.21			1.25	1.46	18.75	3.83	6.04		16.88	5.04	1.46

23

Table 9. Continued.

| | | | | Sampling Location | | | | | | | | | | | | | | | | | | | | | | | | | | | | | |
Species	Frequency	Avg	Std Dev	1*	2	3	5	6	7	8	10	11	12	13	14	15	16	17	18	19	20	21	22	23	24	25	26	27	28	29	30	A1	A2
Ilex opaca	3.33	0.15	0.8																						4.38								
Ilex vomitoria	16.67	1.02	3.37								16.25				1.25						1.25	2.5		9.38								
Ipomoea sagittata	20	1.04	4.11								2.54											1.25	1.25	22.5	2.5					1.25			
Ipomoea sp.	3.33	N/A	N/A	P																												
Juncus canadensis	13.33	0.57	1.82		2.71		6.25																			7.71						
Juncus roemerianus	40	10.1	17.73		27.71		3.75				22.29				51.46			9.58		2.5		32.71	52.5	32.71					0.21	55.83		11.88
Juncus sp.	6.67	0.05	0.23					1.25																		0.21						
Juniperus virginiana	3.33	0.07	0.37																						2							
Lactuca canadensis	3.33	0.01	0.04		0.21																											
Lythrum lineare	6.67	0.13	0.5																			1.25									2.5		
Melothria pendula	3.33	0.04	0.23								1.25																						
Mikania scandens	26.67	1.45	3.12		11.88		6.67								6.88							1.46		5.21	1.25					1.29		
Mitchella repens	3.33	0.32	1.75																						9.58							
Morella cerifera	40	0.91	1.56		1.25			6.25			2.5							2.5		2.71		3.13				1.46			0.42	1.25	1.25	
Muhlenbergia capillaris	3.33	0.22	1.18																									6.46				
Oenothera humifusa	60	2.46	2.59		0.21	7.5		5.42	5.46	4.38	1.25	6.46	5.25		7.5	4.63		2.96	1.46	3.75					2.71	4.58		4.21	1.67		4.46	
Opuntia humifusa	3.33	0.09	0.49																										2.71				
Opuntia sp.	13.33	0.25	0.9			4.79							0.83			0.63						1.25											
Osmanthus americanus	6.67	0.03	0.11																						0.42			0.46				
Oxypolis sp.	3.33	0.01	0.04		0.21																											
Panicum amarum	23.33	1.6	5					2.54	0.13			22.5		1.25			1.25	16.46											
Panicum sp.	6.67	0.2	0.87																			4.63						1.25				
Parthenocissus quinquefolia	23.33	2.55	6.83	P							6.67							1.67				14.38		22.71	3.33							27.71
Paspalum vaginatum	10	0.4	1.76				1.25																9.58							1.25		
Passiflora lutea	3.33	0.01	0.08																						0.42							
Persea borbonia	3.33	0.01	0.04														0.21															
Phyla nodiflora	16.67	0.36	1.08		0.04															2.5		1.46		5.21	1.46							
Physalis viscosa	40	0.55	0.99			0.42		1.25	1.25			3.75	0.08	0.21			1.25			1.25	2.92					0.08		1.46				
Pinus taeda	3.33	0.01	0.04																							0.21					
Polygonum sp.	6.67	0.17	0.75		3.96																				1.25							
Polystichum acrostichoides	3.33	0.04	0.23																						1.25							
Potentilla canadensis	3.33	0.05	0.31																								1.71				
Pteridium aquilinum	3.33	0.62	3.39																								18.54				
Quercus virginiana	6.67	0.41	1.58																						6.67		5.75				
Rhynchospora colorata	10	0.1	0.34																	0.21		1.25			1.46							
Rhynchospora sp.	6.67	0.06	0.24																											0.42	1.25

Table 9. Continued.

Species	Frequency	Avg	Std Dev	1*	2	3	5	6	7	8	10	11	12	13	14	15	16	17	18	19	20	21	22	23	24	25	26	27	28	29	30	A1	A2
Rubus cuneifolius	6.67	0.32	1.33		6.68												2.71																	
Rubus sp.	3.33	0.04	0.23																							1.25								
Rubus trivialis	26.67	0.67	1.78	P				3.75							0.21			1.25				8.75	2.5										1.88
Sanicula canadensis	3.33	0.05	0.27								1.67														1.46								
Schizachyrium scoparium var litorale	13.33	0.18	0.47					1.67										1.25				1.25										1.25
Schoenoplectus americanus	13.33	0.36	1.17		5.83						2.5											1.25			1.25								
Setaria parviflora	3.33	0.01	0.04																	0.21													
Smilax sp.	26.67	2.65	5.94									1.25																	11.04			4.38		21.67
Solidago sempervirens	36.67	1.66	3.47	P			15.63	4.17	1.25			1.88								1.25		1.25				7.71			3.75	8.96	2.5	1.25	
Solidago sp.	13.33	0.42	1.8					1.25														9.79							1.25					0.21
Spartina patens	73.33	16.43	19.36		28.96		50	29.38	8.17		8.33	41.67		5	47.5			4.38		57.92	29.38	21.25	8.13	23.75		20.63	3.96		12.08	66.67	13.54	0.21	6.88
Spiranthes sp.	3.33	0.01	0.04				0.21																											
Strophostyles helvola	13.33	0.26	0.93								0.42						4.38													0.25			2.79	
Thelypteris sp.	3.33	0.24	1.29																						7.08									
Toxicodendron radicans	33.33	7.13	14.78	P	6.67						3.96							20.83				49.79	3.75	37.5	17.5							22.08		51.67
Typha sp.	3.33	0.04	0.23		1.25																													
Uniola paniculata	50	16.42	21.45			49.79		5.21	41.46	38.96		11.04	51.88	32.5		63.75	32.08		35.83	2.5	13.33						57.92		15.83			40.63	
Vaccinium stamineum	3.33	0.04	0.23																										1.25					
Vitis rotundifolia	10	0.47	1.7																						1.25				4.38					8.33
Unidentified																																	
Asteraceae	10	0.31	1.21										5.83												0.21			3.33					
Cyperaceae	13.33	0.19	0.75								0.21													1.25	3.96					0.21			
Fabaceae	10	0.06	0.23					0.21	0.21																1.25								
Lamiaceae	3.33	0.08	0.46					2.5																									
Magnoliopsida	10	0.15	0.57					2.92								1.25									0.42								
Poaceae	30	0.74	1.72		3.75	0.25									2.5			1.25		1.25					1.25	7.92			3.75		0.42		6.25
Ground Condition																																	
Bare ground	76.67	29.67	29.06		12.29	71.67		4.58	50	69.79	3.13	35.83	53.96	41.25		63.75	79.17	5.21	71.67	27.5	38.54					55.42	69.58	1.25	54.79	21.04		56.67	1.25
Exposed humus	20	1.89	5.31				2.71				1.25				0.42							16.67	16.67								18.96		
Leaf litter or duff	96.67	64.02	27.57		87.71	32.08	94.38	44.17	51.92	40	93.54	75.63	57.92	56.88	95.42	51.88	30.42	94.58	28.96	68.96	54.79	97.5	81.46	97.5	88.33	28.75	42.08	94.58	71.25	86.25	36.71	96.46	
Upland non-vascular plants or lichens	10	2.44	12.18					66.67																								0.21	

* Species identified with a "P" at Sampling Location 1 were identified as present, but due to logistical issues at this location, further measurements were unable to be collected.

Literature Cited

Bechtold, W. A. and P. L. Patterson, (eds.). 2005. The enhanced forest inventory and analysis program — national sampling design and estimation procedures. General Technical Report SRS-80. USDA Forest Service, Southern Research Station, Asheville, NC. 85 pp.

DeVivo, J. C., C. J. Wright, M. W. Byrne, E. DiDonato, and T. Curtis. 2008. Vital signs monitoring in the Southeast Coast Inventory & Monitoring Network. Natural Resource Report NPS/SECN/NRR—2008/061. USDI National Park Service, Fort Collins, CO, USA.

Federal Geographic Data Committee. 2008. National vegetation classification standard, version 2. FGDC-STD-005-2008. Available online: http://www.fgdc.gov/standards/project/FGDC-standards-projects/vegetation.

Foster, D. R., G. Motzkin, and B. Slater. 1998. Land-use history as long-term broad-scale disturbance: regional forest dynamics in central New England. Ecosystems: 1:96-119.

NPSpecies - The National Park Service Biodiversity Database. Secure online version. https://science1.nature.nps.gov/npspecies/web/main/start (Park list: accessed 1/13/2011).

Peet R. K., T. R. Wentworth, and P. S White. 1998. A flexible, multipurpose method for recording vegetation composition and structure. Castanea 63:262-274.

Theobald, D. M., D. L. Stevens, D. White, N. S. Urquhart, A. R. Olsen, and J. B. Norman. 2007. Using GIS to generate spatially balanced random survey designs for natural resource applications Environmental Management 40:134-146.

Turner, II, B. L., W. C. Clark, R. W. Kates, J. F. Richards, J. T. Mathews, and W. B. Meyer, (eds.). 1990. The earth as transformed by human action: Global and regional changes in the biosphere over the past 300 years. Cambridge University Press, Cambridge, UK.

Appendix A. Plant species known to occur at CALO.

Table A-1. Vascular plant species known occur at Cape Lookout National Seashore (NPSpecies 2011) and species detected during 2010 monitoring efforts.

Family	Species	NPSpecies	This Study
Aceraceae	*Acer rubrum*	X	
Acoraceae	*Acorus americanus*	X	
Agavaceae	*Yucca aloifolia*	X	X
Agavaceae	*Yucca gloriosa*	X	X
Aizoaceae	*Sesuvium maritimum*	X	
Aizoaceae	*Sesuvium portulacastrum*	X	
Alismataceae	*Sagittaria falcata*	X	
Alismataceae	*Sagittaria lancifolia*	X	
Alismataceae	*Sagittaria latifolia*	X	
Amaranthaceae	*Amaranthus cannabinus*	X	
Amaranthaceae	*Amaranthus hybridus*	X	
Amaranthaceae	*Amaranthus pumilus*	X	
Amaranthaceae	*Iresine rhizomatosa*	X	
Anacardiaceae	*Rhus copallinum*	X	X
Anacardiaceae	*Toxicodendron pubescens*	X	
Anacardiaceae	*Toxicodendron radicans*	X	X
Annonaceae	*Asimina parviflora*	X	
Apiaceae	*Centella asiatica*	X	X
Apiaceae	*Centella erecta*	X	
Apiaceae	*Cicuta curtissii*	X	
Apiaceae	*Cicuta maculata*	X	
Apiaceae	*Hydrocotyle bonariensis*	X	X
Apiaceae	*Hydrocotyle umbellata*	X	X
Apiaceae	*Hydrocotyle verticillata*	X	
Apiaceae	*Lilaeopsis chinensis*	X	
Apiaceae	*Ptilimnium capillaceum*	X	X
Apiaceae	*Sanicula canadensis*	X	X
Apiaceae	*Spermolepis divaricata*	X	
Apocynaceae	*Apocynum cannabinum*	X	
Aquifoliaceae	*Ilex cassine*	X	
Aquifoliaceae	*Ilex glabra*	X	X
Aquifoliaceae	*Ilex opaca*	X	X
Aquifoliaceae	*Ilex vomitoria*	X	X
Araliaceae	*Aralia spinosa*	X	
Arecaceae	*Sabal minor*	X	
Asclepiadaceae	*Asclepias lanceolata*	X	
Asclepiadaceae	*Cynanchum angustifolium*	X	X
Asclepiadaceae	*Matelea gonocarpos*	X	
Asclepiadaceae	*Matelea suberosa*	X	
Aspleniaceae	*Asplenium platyneuron*	X	X
Aspleniaceae	*Asplenium X ebenoides*	X	
Asteraceae	*Achillea millefolium*	X	
Asteraceae	*Achillea millefolium ssp. lanulosa*	X	
Asteraceae	*Ambrosia artemisiifolia*	X	X

Table A-1. Continued.

Family	Species	NPSpecies	This Study
Asteraceae	*Ampelaster carolinianus*	X	
Asteraceae	*Aster subulatus var. subulatus*	X	
Asteraceae	*Baccharis angustifolia*	X	X
Asteraceae	*Baccharis halimifolia*	X	X
Asteraceae	*Bidens bipinnata*	X	
Asteraceae	*Bidens laevis*	X	
Asteraceae	*Borrichia frutescens*	X	X
Asteraceae	*Chrysopsis graminifolia*	X	
Asteraceae	*Cirsium horridulum*	X	X
Asteraceae	*Cirsium spinosissimum*	X	
Asteraceae	*Conyza canadensis*	X	X
Asteraceae	*Conyza canadensis var. canadensis*	X	
Asteraceae	*Conyza canadensis var. pusilla*	X	
Asteraceae	*Coreopsis gladiata*	X	
Asteraceae	*Coreopsis lanceolata*	X	
Asteraceae	*Eclipta prostrata*	X	
Asteraceae	*Elephantopus carolinianus*	X	
Asteraceae	*Elephantopus nudatus*	X	
Asteraceae	*Elephantopus tomentosus*	X	X
Asteraceae	*Erechtites hieraciifolia*	X	X
Asteraceae	*Erigeron annuus*	X	
Asteraceae	*Erigeron canadensis*	X	
Asteraceae	*Erigeron pusillus*	X	
Asteraceae	*Erigeron quercifolius*	X	
Asteraceae	*Eupatorium anomalum*	X	
Asteraceae	*Eupatorium aromaticum*	X	
Asteraceae	*Eupatorium capillifolium*	X	X
Asteraceae	*Eupatorium dubium*	X	
Asteraceae	*Eupatorium hyssopifolium var. laciniatum*	X	
Asteraceae	*Eupatorium leucolepis*	X	
Asteraceae	*Eupatorium mohrii*	X	
Asteraceae	*Eupatorium pilosum*	X	
Asteraceae	*Eupatorium serotinum*	X	
Asteraceae	*Euthamia minor*	X	
Asteraceae	*Euthamia tenuifolia*	X	
Asteraceae	*Gaillardia pulchella*	X	X
Asteraceae	*Gamochaeta purpurea*	X	
Asteraceae	*Gnaphalium obtusifolium*	X	
Asteraceae	*Gnaphalium purpureum var. americanum*	X	
Asteraceae	*Gnaphalium purpureum var. spathulatum*	X	
Asteraceae	*Heterotheca subaxillaris*	X	X
Asteraceae	*Hieracium gronovii*	X	
Asteraceae	*Iva frutescens*	X	X
Asteraceae	*Iva imbricata*	X	
Asteraceae	*Krigia virginica*	X	
Asteraceae	*Lactuca canadensis*	X	X
Asteraceae	*Lactuca graminifolia*	X	

Table A-1. Continued.

Family	Species	NPSpecies	This Study
Asteraceae	*Leucanthemum vulgare*	X	
Asteraceae	*Liatris graminifolia*	X	
Asteraceae	*Mikania scandens*	X	X
Asteraceae	*Pluchea camphorata*	X	X
Asteraceae	*Pluchea carolinensis*	X	
Asteraceae	*Pluchea foetida*	X	
Asteraceae	*Pluchea purpurascens*	X	
Asteraceae	*Pluchea rosea*	X	X
Asteraceae	*Pterocaulon virgatum*	X	
Asteraceae	*Pyrrhopappus carolinianus*	X	
Asteraceae	*Rudbeckia hirta*	X	
Asteraceae	*Senecio vulgaris*	X	
Asteraceae	*Solidago fistulosa*	X	
Asteraceae	*Solidago microcephala*	X	
Asteraceae	*Solidago odora*	X	
Asteraceae	*Solidago sempervirens*	X	X
Asteraceae	*Sonchus asper*	X	
Asteraceae	*Sonchus oleraceus*	X	
Asteraceae	*Symphyotrichum racemosum*	X	
Asteraceae	*Symphyotrichum subulatum*	X	
Asteraceae	*Symphyotrichum tenuifolium*	X	
Asteraceae	*Taraxacum officinale*	X	
Asteraceae	*Xanthium strumarium*	X	
Betulaceae	*Carpinus caroliniana*	X	X
Bignoniaceae	*Campsis radicans*		X
Bignoniaceae	*Catalpa bignonioides*	X	
Blechnaceae	*Woodwardia virginica*	X	
Boraginaceae	*Heliotropium curassavicum*	X	
Brassicaceae	*Cakile edentula*	X	
Brassicaceae	*Cakile harperi*	X	
Brassicaceae	*Cardamine hirsuta*	X	
Brassicaceae	*Lepidium virginicum*	X	X
Brassicaceae	*Raphanus raphanistrum*	X	
Bromeliaceae	*Tillandsia usneoides*	X	
Buddlejaceae	*Polypremum procumbens*	X	
Cactaceae	*Opuntia ficus-indica*	X	
Cactaceae	*Opuntia humifusa*	X	X
Cactaceae	*Opuntia pusilla*	X	
Campanulaceae	*Specularia perfoliata*	X	
Campanulaceae	*Triodanis perfoliata*	X	
Cannaceae	*Canna X generalis*	X	
Caprifoliaceae	*Lonicera japonica*	X	
Caprifoliaceae	*Lonicera sempervirens*	X	
Caryophyllaceae	*Anychiastrum baldwinii*	X	
Caryophyllaceae	*Arenaria lanuginosa*	X	
Caryophyllaceae	*Arenaria serpyllifolia*	X	
Caryophyllaceae	*Cerastium glomeratum*	X	

Table A-1. Continued.

Family	Species	NPSpecies	This Study
Caryophyllaceae	*Holosteum umbellatum*	X	
Caryophyllaceae	*Paronychia riparia*	X	
Caryophyllaceae	*Sagina decumbens*	X	
Caryophyllaceae	*Silene antirrhina*	X	
Caryophyllaceae	*Spergularia salina*	X	
Caryophyllaceae	*Stellaria media*	X	
Celastraceae	*Euonymus patens*	X	
Ceratophyllaceae	*Ceratophyllum demersum*	X	
Chenopodiaceae	*Atriplex cristata*	X	
Chenopodiaceae	*Atriplex patula*	X	
Chenopodiaceae	*Atriplex patula ssp. hastata*	X	
Chenopodiaceae	*Atriplex patula var. hastata*	X	
Chenopodiaceae	*Chenopodium ambrosioides*	X	
Chenopodiaceae	*Chenopodium botrys*	X	
Chenopodiaceae	*Chenopodium glaucum*	X	
Chenopodiaceae	*Chenopodium opulifolium*	X	
Chenopodiaceae	*Salicornia bigelovii*	X	
Chenopodiaceae	*Salicornia maritima*	X	
Chenopodiaceae	*Salicornia virginica*	X	
Chenopodiaceae	*Salsola kali*	X	
Chenopodiaceae	*Sarcocornia perennis*	X	
Chenopodiaceae	*Suaeda linearis*	X	
Cistaceae	*Helianthemum corymbosum*	X	
Cistaceae	*Helianthemum georgianum*	X	
Cistaceae	*Lechea leggettii*	X	
Cistaceae	*Lechea mucronata*	X	
Clusiaceae	*Hypericum crux-andreae*	X	
Clusiaceae	*Hypericum gentianoides*	X	
Clusiaceae	*Hypericum hypericoides*	X	X
Clusiaceae	*Hypericum mutilum*	X	
Clusiaceae	*Hypericum perforatum*	X	
Clusiaceae	*Triadenum virginicum*	X	
Commelinaceae	*Commelina angustifolia*	X	
Commelinaceae	*Commelina erecta*	X	X
Commelinaceae	*Tradescantia ohiensis*	X	
Convolvulaceae	*Calystegia sepium*	X	
Convolvulaceae	*Dichondra carolinensis*	X	
Convolvulaceae	*Ipomoea batatas*	X	
Convolvulaceae	*Ipomoea lacunosa*	X	
Convolvulaceae	*Ipomoea pandurata*	X	
Convolvulaceae	*Ipomoea sagittata*	X	X
Cornaceae	*Cornus florida*	X	
Cornaceae	*Cornus foemina*	X	X
Cucurbitaceae	*Cucurbita pepo*	X	
Cucurbitaceae	*Lagenaria siceraria*	X	
Cucurbitaceae	*Melothria pendula*	X	X

Table A-1. Continued.

Family	Species	NPSpecies	This Study
Cupressaceae	*Juniperus silicicola*	X	
Cupressaceae	*Juniperus virginiana*	X	X
Cuscutaceae	*Cuscuta arvensis*	X	
Cuscutaceae	*Cuscuta gronovii*	X	
Cyperaceae	*Bolboschoenus robustus*	X	X
Cyperaceae	*Bulbostylis capillaris*	X	
Cyperaceae	*Bulbostylis ciliatifolia*	X	
Cyperaceae	*Bulbostylis stenophylla*	X	
Cyperaceae	*Carex alata*	X	
Cyperaceae	*Carex albolutescens*	X	
Cyperaceae	*Carex nigromarginata*	X	
Cyperaceae	*Carex nigromarginata var. floridana*	X	
Cyperaceae	*Cladium jamaicense*	X	X
Cyperaceae	*Cyperus bipartitus*	X	
Cyperaceae	*Cyperus croceus*	X	
Cyperaceae	*Cyperus cylindricus*	X	
Cyperaceae	*Cyperus filicinus*	X	
Cyperaceae	*Cyperus flavescens*	X	
Cyperaceae	*Cyperus haspan*	X	X
Cyperaceae	*Cyperus odoratus*	X	
Cyperaceae	*Cyperus ovatus*	X	
Cyperaceae	*Cyperus polystachyos*	X	
Cyperaceae	*Cyperus polystachyos var. texensis*	X	
Cyperaceae	*Cyperus retrofractus*	X	
Cyperaceae	*Cyperus retrorsus*	X	
Cyperaceae	*Cyperus strigosus*	X	
Cyperaceae	*Cyperus tetragonus*	X	
Cyperaceae	*Dulichium arundinaceum*	X	
Cyperaceae	*Eleocharis albida*	X	
Cyperaceae	*Eleocharis fallax*	X	
Cyperaceae	*Eleocharis flavescens*	X	
Cyperaceae	*Eleocharis microcarpa*	X	
Cyperaceae	*Eleocharis montevidensis*	X	
Cyperaceae	*Eleocharis ochreata*	X	
Cyperaceae	*Eleocharis olivacea*	X	
Cyperaceae	*Eleocharis robbinsii*	X	
Cyperaceae	*Eleocharis rostellata*	X	
Cyperaceae	*Fimbristylis autumnalis*	X	
Cyperaceae	*Fimbristylis caroliniana*	X	X
Cyperaceae	*Fimbristylis castanea*	X	
Cyperaceae	*Fimbristylis dichotoma*	X	
Cyperaceae	*Fimbristylis thermalis*	X	
Cyperaceae	*Fuirena breviseta*	X	
Cyperaceae	*Fuirena squarrosa*	X	
Cyperaceae	*Rhynchospora caduca*	X	
Cyperaceae	*Rhynchospora colorata*	X	X
Cyperaceae	*Rhynchospora glomerata*	X	

Table A-1. Continued.

Family	Species	NPSpecies	This Study
Cyperaceae	*Rhynchospora latifolia*	X	
Cyperaceae	*Rhynchospora odorata*	X	
Cyperaceae	*Schoenoplectus americanus*	X	X
Cyperaceae	*Schoenoplectus tabernaemontani*	X	
Cyperaceae	*Scirpus acutus*	X	
Cyperaceae	*Scirpus americanus*	X	
Cyperaceae	*Scleria triglomerata*	X	
Cyperaceae	*Scleria verticillata*	X	X
Dennstaedtiaceae	*Pteridium aquilinum*	X	X
Dryopteridaceae	*Onoclea sensibilis*	X	
Dryopteridaceae	*Polystichum acrostichoides*		X
Ebenaceae	*Diospyros virginiana*	X	X
Ericaceae	*Gaylussacia dumosa*		X
Ericaceae	*Lyonia lucida*	X	
Ericaceae	*Vaccinium arboreum*	X	X
Ericaceae	*Vaccinium corymbosum*	X	X
Ericaceae	*Vaccinium fuscatum*	X	
Ericaceae	*Vaccinium myrsinites*	X	
Ericaceae	*Vaccinium stamineum*	X	X
Ericaceae	*Vaccinium tenellum*	X	
Ericaceae	*Vaccinium virgatum*	X	
Euphorbiaceae	*Acalypha gracilens*	X	
Euphorbiaceae	*Chamaesyce maculata*	X	
Euphorbiaceae	*Chamaesyce nutans*	X	
Euphorbiaceae	*Chamaesyce polygonifolia*	X	X
Euphorbiaceae	*Cnidoscolus stimulosus*	X	X
Euphorbiaceae	*Croton glandulosus*	X	
Euphorbiaceae	*Croton glandulosus var. septentrionalis*	X	
Euphorbiaceae	*Croton punctatus*	X	X
Euphorbiaceae	*Ricinus communis*	X	
Fabaceae	*Apios americana*	X	
Fabaceae	*Cassia chamaecrista*	X	
Fabaceae	*Cassia nictitans*	X	
Fabaceae	*Centrosema virginianum*		X
Fabaceae	*Clitoria mariana*	X	
Fabaceae	*Crotalaria rotundifolia*	X	
Fabaceae	*Desmodium paniculatum*	X	
Fabaceae	*Desmodium perplexum*	X	
Fabaceae	*Desmodium strictum*	X	
Fabaceae	*Galactia volubilis*	X	
Fabaceae	*Kummerowia striata*	X	
Fabaceae	*Lespedeza cuneata*	X	
Fabaceae	*Lespedeza virginica*	X	
Fabaceae	*Mimosa microphylla*	X	
Fabaceae	*Robinia pseudoacacia*	X	
Fabaceae	*Sesbania punicea*	X	
Fabaceae	*Strophostyles helvola*	X	X

Table A-1. Continued.

Family	Species	NPSpecies	This Study
Fabaceae	*Strophostyles umbellata*	X	
Fabaceae	*Trifolium aureum*	X	
Fabaceae	*Trifolium dubium*	X	
Fabaceae	*Trifolium repens*	X	
Fagaceae	*Quercus falcata*	X	
Fagaceae	*Quercus laurifolia*	X	X
Fagaceae	*Quercus nigra*	X	X
Fagaceae	*Quercus phellos*	X	
Fagaceae	*Quercus stellata*	X	
Fagaceae	*Quercus virginiana*	X	X
Gentianaceae	*Sabatia calycina*		X
Gentianaceae	*Sabatia campanulata*		X
Gentianaceae	*Sabatia stellaris*	X	
Geraniaceae	*Geranium carolinianum*	X	
Haloragaceae	*Myriophyllum verticillatum*	X	
Haloragaceae	*Proserpinaca palustris*	X	
Haloragaceae	*Proserpinaca pectinata*	X	
Hamamelidaceae	*Hamamelis virginiana*	X	
Iridaceae	*Gladiolus X gandavensis*	X	
Iridaceae	*Hypoxis hirsuta*	X	
Iridaceae	*Sisyrinchium atlanticum*	X	
Iridaceae	*Sisyrinchium mucronatum*	X	
Iridaceae	*Sisyrinchium mucronatum var. atlanticum*	X	
Iridaceae	*Sisyrinchium rosulatum*	X	
Juglandaceae	*Carya glabra*	X	
Juncaceae	*Juncus biflorus*	X	
Juncaceae	*Juncus bufonius*	X	
Juncaceae	*Juncus canadensis*	X	X
Juncaceae	*Juncus coriaceus*	X	
Juncaceae	*Juncus dichotomus*	X	
Juncaceae	*Juncus effusus*	X	
Juncaceae	*Juncus marginatus*	X	X
Juncaceae	*Juncus megacephalus*	X	
Juncaceae	*Juncus roemerianus*	X	X
Juncaceae	*Juncus scirpoides*	X	
Juncaceae	*Juncus tenuis*	X	
Juncaginaceae	*Triglochin striata*	X	
Lamiaceae	*Lamium amplexicaule*	X	
Lamiaceae	*Lycopus virginicus*	X	
Lamiaceae	*Marrubium vulgare*	X	
Lamiaceae	*Monarda punctata*	X	
Lamiaceae	*Scutellaria integrifolia*	X	
Lamiaceae	*Teucrium canadense*	X	X
Lamiaceae	*Trichostema dichotomum*	X	
Lauraceae	*Persea borbonia*	X	X
Lauraceae	*Persea palustris*	X	
Lauraceae	*Sassafras albidum*	X	

Table A-1. Continued.

Family	Species	NPSpecies	This Study
Lent bulariaceae	*Utricularia purpurea*	X	
Lent bulariaceae	*Utricularia subulata*	X	
Liliaceae	*Allium canadense*	X	
Liliaceae	*Allium vineale*	X	
Liliaceae	*Nothoscordum bivalve*	X	
Linaceae	*Linum floridanum var. floridanum*	X	
Linaceae	*Linum medium*	X	
Linaceae	*Linum medium var. medium*	X	
Linaceae	*Linum virginianum*	X	
Loganiaceae	*Gelsemium sempervirens*	X	X
Loganiaceae	*Mitreola petiolata*	X	
Lythraceae	*Ammannia coccinea*	X	
Lythraceae	*Ammannia latifolia*	X	
Lythraceae	*Cuphea carthagenensis*	X	
Lythraceae	*Decodon verticillatus*	X	
Lythraceae	*Lythrum lineare*	X	X
Magnoliaceae	*Magnolia grandiflora*		X
Magnoliaceae	*Magnolia virginiana*	X	
Malvaceae	*Hibiscus moscheutos*	X	
Malvaceae	*Kosteletzkya virginica*	X	X
Malvaceae	*Sida rhombifolia*	X	
Melastomataceae	*Rhexia mariana*	X	
Meliaceae	*Melia azedarach*	X	
Molluginaceae	*Mollugo verticillata*	X	
Moraceae	*Ficus carica*	X	
Moraceae	*Maclura pomifera*	X	
Moraceae	*Morus rubra*	X	
Myricaceae	*Morella caroliniensis*	X	
Myricaceae	*Morella cerifera*	X	X
Myricaceae	*Myrica gale*	X	
Nyssaceae	*Nyssa ogeche*	X	
Nyssaceae	*Nyssa sylvatica*	X	
Nyssaceae	*Nyssa sylvatica var. biflora*	X	
Oleaceae	*Fraxinus caroliniana*		X
Oleaceae	*Osmanthus americanus*	X	X
Onagraceae	*Gaura angustifolia*	X	X
Onagraceae	*Gaura biennis*	X	
Onagraceae	*Gaura mollis*	X	
Onagraceae	*Kneiffia arenicola*	X	
Onagraceae	*Ludwigia alata*	X	X
Onagraceae	*Ludwigia maritima*	X	
Onagraceae	*Ludwigia microcarpa*	X	
Onagraceae	*Ludwigia palustris*	X	
Onagraceae	*Ludwigia repens*	X	X
Onagraceae	*Ludwigia virgata*	X	
Onagraceae	*Oenothera biennis*	X	X
Onagraceae	*Oenothera fruticosa*	X	

Table A-1. Continued.

Family	Species	NPSpecies	This Study
Onagraceae	*Oenothera humifusa*	X	X
Onagraceae	*Oenothera laciniata*	X	
Onagraceae	*Oenothera parviflora*	X	
Ophioglossaceae	*Ophioglossum petiolatum*	X	
Orchidaceae	*Corallorrhiza wisteriana*	X	
Orchidaceae	*Spiranthes gracilis*	X	
Orchidaceae	*Spiranthes laciniata*	X	
Orchidaceae	*Spiranthes ovalis*	X	
Orchidaceae	*Spiranthes vernalis*	X	X
Osmundaceae	*Osmunda regalis*	X	X
Osmundaceae	*Osmunda regalis var. spectabilis*	X	
Oxalidaceae	*Oxalis rubra*	X	
Oxalidaceae	*Oxalis stricta*	X	X
Oxalidaceae	*Oxalis violacea*	X	
Passifloraceae	*Passiflora incarnata*	X	
Passifloraceae	*Passiflora lutea*	X	X
Phytolaccaceae	*Phytolacca americana*	X	X
Phytolaccaceae	*Phytolacca decandra*	X	
Pinaceae	*Pinus taeda*	X	X
Plantaginaceae	*Plantago heterophylla*	X	
Plantaginaceae	*Plantago lanceolata*	X	
Plantaginaceae	*Plantago virginica*	X	
Plumbaginaceae	*Limonium carolinianum*	X	
Poaceae	*Agrostis stolonifera*	X	
Poaceae	*Ammophila breviligulata*	X	
Poaceae	*Andropogon glomeratus*	X	X
Poaceae	*Andropogon glomeratus var. glomeratus*		X
Poaceae	*Andropogon virginicus*	X	
Poaceae	*Andropogon virginicus var. glaucopsis*	X	
Poaceae	*Andropogon virginicus var. virginicus*	X	
Poaceae	*Arthraxon hispidus var. cryptatherus*	X	
Poaceae	*Axonopus fissifolius*	X	
Poaceae	*Briza minor*	X	
Poaceae	*Bromus japonicus*	X	
Poaceae	*Bromus rigidus*	X	
Poaceae	*Cenchrus longispinus*	X	
Poaceae	*Cenchrus spinifex*	X	
Poaceae	*Cenchrus tribuloides*	X	X
Poaceae	*Chasmanthium laxum*	X	X
Poaceae	*Cynodon dactylon*	X	
Poaceae	*Dactylus glomerata*	X	
Poaceae	*Dichanthelium aciculare*	X	
Poaceae	*Dichanthelium acuminatum var. fasciculatum*	X	
Poaceae	*Dichanthelium commutatum*	X	
Poaceae	*Dichanthelium dichotomum var. dichotomum*	X	
Poaceae	*Dichanthelium latifolium*	X	
Poaceae	*Dichanthelium laxiflorum*	X	

Table A-1. Continued.

Family	Species	NPSpecies	This Study
Poaceae	*Dichanthelium sabulorum var. patulum*	X	
Poaceae	*Dichanthelium scabriusculum*	X	
Poaceae	*Dichanthelium scoparium*	X	
Poaceae	*Dichanthelium spretum*	X	
Poaceae	*Digitaria filiformis*	X	
Poaceae	*Digitaria sanguinalis*	X	
Poaceae	*Distichlis spicata*	X	X
Poaceae	*Echinochloa crus-galli*	X	
Poaceae	*Echinochloa walteri*	X	
Poaceae	*Eleusine indica*	X	
Poaceae	*Elymus virginicus*	X	X
Poaceae	*Elymus virginicus var. halophilus*	X	
Poaceae	*Eragrostis curvula*	X	
Poaceae	*Eragrostis elliottii*	X	
Poaceae	*Eragrostis pectinacea*	X	
Poaceae	*Eragrostis pilosa*	X	
Poaceae	*Eragrostis refracta*	X	
Poaceae	*Eragrostis spectabilis*	X	
Poaceae	*Eremochloa ophiuroides*	X	X
Poaceae	*Eustachys petraea*	X	X
Poaceae	*Festuca octoflora*	X	
Poaceae	*Festuca rubra*	X	
Poaceae	*Glyceria acutiflora*	X	
Poaceae	*Hordeum pusillum*	X	
Poaceae	*Lolium multiflorum*	X	
Poaceae	*Lolium perenne*	X	
Poaceae	*Lolium pratense*	X	
Poaceae	*Melica mutica*	X	X
Poaceae	*Muhlenbergia capillaris*	X	X
Poaceae	*Muhlenbergia capillaris var. filipes*	X	
Poaceae	*Oplismenus hirtellus*	X	
Poaceae	*Panicum acuminatum*	X	
Poaceae	*Panicum amarum*	X	X
Poaceae	*Panicum anceps*	X	
Poaceae	*Panicum dichotomiflorum*	X	
Poaceae	*Panicum lancearium*	X	
Poaceae	*Panicum longifolium*	X	
Poaceae	*Panicum portoricense var. portoricense*	X	
Poaceae	*Panicum rigidulum var. rigidulum*	X	
Poaceae	*Panicum sphaerocarpon*	X	
Poaceae	*Panicum verrucosum*	X	
Poaceae	*Panicum virgatum*	X	
Poaceae	*Panicum virgatum var. virgatum*	X	
Poaceae	*Parapholis incurva*	X	
Poaceae	*Paspalum distichum*	X	
Poaceae	*Paspalum floridanum*	X	
Poaceae	*Paspalum laeve*	X	

Table A-1. Continued.

Family	Species	NPSpecies	This Study
Poaceae	*Paspalum notatum*	X	
Poaceae	*Paspalum setaceum*	X	
Poaceae	*Paspalum urvillei*	X	X
Poaceae	*Paspalum vaginatum*	X	X
Poaceae	*Phalaris caroliniana*	X	
Poaceae	*Phleum pratense*	X	
Poaceae	*Phragmites australis*		X
Poaceae	*Piptochaetium avenaceum*	X	
Poaceae	*Poa annua*	X	
Poaceae	*Poa pratensis*	X	
Poaceae	*Polypogon monspeliensis*	X	
Poaceae	*Saccharum giganteum*	X	
Poaceae	*Sacciolepis striata*	X	
Poaceae	*Schizachyrium scoparium var. litoralle*	X	X
Poaceae	*Setaria glauca*	X	
Poaceae	*Setaria magna*	X	X
Poaceae	*Setaria parviflora*	X	X
Poaceae	*Sorghastrum elliottii*	X	
Poaceae	*Spartina alterniflora*	X	
Poaceae	*Spartina cynosuroides*	X	
Poaceae	*Spartina patens*	X	X
Poaceae	*Sphenopholis obtusata*	X	
Poaceae	*Sphenopholis pensylvanica*	X	
Poaceae	*Sporobolus indicus*	X	
Poaceae	*Sporobolus poiretii*	X	
Poaceae	*Sporobolus virginicus*	X	X
Poaceae	*Stenotaphrum secundatum*	X	
Poaceae	*Tridens flavus*	X	
Poaceae	*Triplasis purpurea*	X	
Poaceae	*Uniola paniculata*	X	X
Poaceae	*Vulpia myuros*	X	
Poaceae	*Vulpia octoflora*	X	
Poaceae	*Vulpia sciurea*	X	
Polemoniaceae	*Phlox drummondii*	X	
Polygalaceae	*Polygala lutea*	X	
Polygalaceae	*Polygala verticillata*	X	
Polygonaceae	*Polygonum glaucum*	X	
Polygonaceae	*Polygonum lapathifolium*	X	
Polygonaceae	*Polygonum persicaria*	X	
Polygonaceae	*Polygonum punctatum*	X	X
Polygonaceae	*Polygonum punctatum var. confertiflorum*	X	
Polygonaceae	*Polygonum setaceum*	X	
Polygonaceae	*Rumex crispus*	X	
Polygonaceae	*Rumex hastatulus*	X	
Polypodiaceae	*Polypodium polypodioides*	X	
Portulacaceae	*Portulaca oleracea*	X	
Primulaceae	*Samolus floribundus*	X	

Table A-1. Continued.

Family	Species	NPSpecies	This Study
Primulaceae	*Samolus parviflorus*	X	
Ranunculaceae	*Clematis catesbyana*	X	
Ranunculaceae	*Clematis ligusticifolia*	X	
Ranunculaceae	*Myosurus minimus*	X	
Ranunculaceae	*Ranunculus sceleratus*	X	
Rhamnaceae	*Berchemia scandens*	X	X
Rosaceae	*Amelanchier canadensis*	X	
Rosaceae	*Amelanchier obovalis*	X	
Rosaceae	*Potentilla canadensis*		X
Rosaceae	*Prunus angustifolia*	X	
Rosaceae	*Prunus caroliniana*	X	
Rosaceae	*Prunus serotina*	X	
Rosaceae	*Rosa carolina*	X	
Rosaceae	*Rosa multiflora*		X
Rosaceae	*Rosa palustris*	X	X
Rosaceae	*Rubus allegheniensis*	X	
Rosaceae	*Rubus cuneifolius*		X
Rosaceae	*Rubus persistens*	X	
Rosaceae	*Rubus trivialis*	X	X
Rubiaceae	*Diodia teres*	X	X
Rubiaceae	*Diodia virginiana*	X	X
Rubiaceae	*Galium hispidulum*	X	X
Rubiaceae	*Galium obtusum*	X	X
Rubiaceae	*Galium obtusum ssp. obtusum*	X	
Rubiaceae	*Galium pilosum*	X	X
Rubiaceae	*Galium pilosum var. puncticulosum*	X	
Rubiaceae	*Galium tinctorium*		X
Rubiaceae	*Mitchella repens*	X	X
Rubiaceae	*Oldenlandia uniflora*	X	
Ruppiaceae	*Ruppia maritima*	X	
Rutaceae	*Zanthoxylum clava-herculis*	X	
Salicaceae	*Populus alba*	X	
Salicaceae	*Salix caroliniana*	X	
Sapotaceae	*Sideroxylon lycioides*	X	
Sapotaceae	*Sideroxylon tenax*	X	
Saururaceae	*Saururus cernuus*	X	
Scrophulariaceae	*Agalinis maritima*	X	
Scrophulariaceae	*Agalinis purpurea*	X	
Scrophulariaceae	*Aureolaria flava*	X	
Scrophulariaceae	*Aureolaria laevigata*	X	
Scrophulariaceae	*Bacopa monnieri*	X	X
Scrophulariaceae	*Buchnera americana*	X	
Scrophulariaceae	*Gerardia maritima*	X	
Scrophulariaceae	*Gratiola virginiana*	X	
Scrophulariaceae	*Nuttallanthus canadensis*	X	
Scrophulariaceae	*Verbascum thapsus*	X	
Scrophulariaceae	*Veronica arvensis*	X	

Table A-1. Continued.

Family	Species	NPSpecies	This Study
Scrophulariaceae	*Veronica peregrina*	X	
Simaroubaceae	*Ailanthus altissima*	X	
Smilacaceae	*Smilax auriculata*	X	
Smilacaceae	*Smilax bona-nox*	X	
Smilacaceae	*Smilax glauca*	X	X
Smilacaceae	*Smilax laurifolia*	X	
Smilacaceae	*Smilax rotundifolia*	X	
Smilacaceae	*Smilax tamnoides*	X	
Solanaceae	*Datura stramonium*	X	
Solanaceae	*Petunia X atkinsiana*	X	
Solanaceae	*Physalis pubescens*	X	
Solanaceae	*Physalis viscosa*	X	X
Solanaceae	*Physalis viscosa ssp. maritima*	X	
Solanaceae	*Physalis walteri*	X	
Solanaceae	*Solanum carolinense*	X	
Solanaceae	*Solanum gracilius*	X	
Solanaceae	*Solanum pseudogracile*	X	
Sparganiaceae	*Sparganium androcladum*	X	
Tamaricaceae	*Tamarix gallica*	X	
Taxodiaceae	*Taxodium distichum*	X	
Thelypteridaceae	*Dryopteris thelypteris*	X	
Thelypteridaceae	*Thelypteris palustris*	X	X
Tiliaceae	*Tilia michauxii*	X	
Typhaceae	*Typha angustifolia*	X	
Typhaceae	*Typha domingensis*	X	
Typhaceae	*Typha latifolia*	X	
Ulmaceae	*Celtis occidentalis*	X	
Urticaceae	*Boehmeria cylindrica*	X	X
Urticaceae	*Parietaria floridana*	X	
Urticaceae	*Parietaria praetermissa*	X	
Urticaceae	*Pilea fontana*	X	
Urticaceae	*Pilea pumila*	X	
Valerianaceae	*Valerianella radiata*	X	
Verbenaceae	*Callicarpa americana*	X	X
Verbenaceae	*Lantana camara*	X	
Verbenaceae	*Phyla nodiflora*	X	X
Verbenaceae	*Verbena polystachya*	X	
Verbenaceae	*Verbena scabra*	X	
Violaceae	*Viola primulifolia*	X	
Viscaceae	*Phoradendron leucarpum*	X	
Vitaceae	*Ampelopsis arborea*	X	X
Vitaceae	*Parthenocissus quinquefolia*	X	X
Vitaceae	*Vitis aestivalis*	X	X
Vitaceae	*Vitis labrusca*	X	
Vitaceae	*Vitis rotundifolia*	X	X
Xyridaceae	*Xyris caroliniana*	X	
Zosteraceae	*Zostera marina*	X	

Appendix B. Plant species detected in macroplots at Cape Lookout National Seashore.

Table B-1. Vascular plant species detected in all macroplot inventories (i.e., across macroplot species composition) at Cape Lookout National Seashore, 2010.

Order	Family	Species	Common Name
Liliales	Agavaceae	*Yucca aloifolia*	aloe yucca
Liliales	Agavaceae	*Yucca gloriosa*	moundlily yucca
Sapindales	Anacardiaceae	*Rhus copallinum*	flameleaf sumac
Sapindales	Anacardiaceae	*Toxicodendron radicans*	eastern poison ivy, poison ivy, poisonivy
Apiales	Apiaceae	*Centella asiatica*	spadeleaf
Apiales	Apiaceae	*Hydrocotyle bonariensis*	largeleaf pennywort
Apiales	Apiaceae	*Hydrocotyle umbellata*	manyflower marshpennywort, umbrella pennyroyal
Apiales	Apiaceae	*Ptilimnium capillaceum*	herbwilliam, threadleaf mockbishopweed
Apiales	Apiaceae	*Sanicula canadensis*	Canada sanicle, Canadian blacksnakeroot
Celastrales	Aquifoliaceae	*Ilex glabra*	inberry, inkberry
Celastrales	Aquifoliaceae	*Ilex opaca*	American holly
Celastrales	Aquifoliaceae	*Ilex vomitoria*	yaupon
Gentianales	Asclepiadaceae	*Cynanchum angustifolium*	gulf coast swallow-wort, Gulf coast swallowwort
Polypodiales	Aspleniaceae	*Asplenium platyneuron*	ebony spleenwort
Asterales	Asteraceae	*Ambrosia artemisiifolia*	annual ragweed, common ragweed, low ragweed
Asterales	Asteraceae	*Baccharis angustifolia*	saltwater false willow
Asterales	Asteraceae	*Baccharis halimifolia*	eastern baccharis, groundseltree
Asterales	Asteraceae	*Borrichia frutescens*	bushy seaoxeye, bushy seaside tansy
Asterales	Asteraceae	*Cirsium horridulum*	yellow thistle
Asterales	Asteraceae	*Conyza canadensis*	Canada horseweed, Canadian horseweed, horseweed
Asterales	Asteraceae	*Elephantopus tomentosus*	hairy elephant's foot
Asterales	Asteraceae	*Erechtites hieraciifolia*	American burnweed
Asterales	Asteraceae	*Eupatorium capillifolium*	dogfennel
Asterales	Asteraceae	*Gaillardia pulchella*	firewheel, Indian blanket, Indianblanket
Asterales	Asteraceae	*Heterotheca subaxillaris*	camphorweed, golden aster
Asterales	Asteraceae	*Iva frutescens*	bigleaf sumpweed, Jesuit's bark
Asterales	Asteraceae	*Lactuca canadensis*	Canada lettuce, Florida blue lettuce, wild lettuce
Asterales	Asteraceae	*Mikania scandens*	climbing hempvine, climbing hempweed
Asterales	Asteraceae	*Pluchea camphorata*	camphor pluchea, camphor weed
Asterales	Asteraceae	*Pluchea rosea*	rosy camphorweed
Asterales	Asteraceae	*Solidago sempervirens*	seaside goldenrod
Fagales	Betulaceae	*Carpinus caroliniana*	American hornbeam, american hornbean
Scrophulariales	Bignoniaceae	*Campsis radicans*	trumpet creeper
Capparales	Brassicaceae	*Lepidium virginicum*	peppergrass, poorman pepperweed, poorman's pepper
Caryophyllales	Cactaceae	*Opuntia humifusa*	devil's-tongue, pricklypear
Theales	Clusiaceae	*Hypericum hypericoides*	St. Andrews cross, St. Andrew's cross
Commelinales	Commelinaceae	*Commelina erecta*	erect dayflower, whitemouth dayflower
Solanales	Convolvulaceae	*Ipomoea sagittata*	saltmarsh morningglory, saltmarsh morning-glory
Cornales	Cornaceae	*Cornus foemina*	stiff dogwood
Violales	Cucurbitaceae	*Melothria pendula*	drooping melonnettle, Guadeloupe cucumber

Table B-1. Continued.

Order	Family	Species	Common Name
Pinales	Cupressaceae	*Juniperus virginiana*	eastern redcedar, eastern red-cedar, red cedar juniper
Cyperales	Cyperaceae	*Bolboschoenus robustus*	sturdy bulrush
Cyperales	Cyperaceae	*Cladium jamaicense*	sawgrass
Cyperales	Cyperaceae	*Cyperus haspan*	haspan flatsedge
Cyperales	Cyperaceae	*Fimbristylis caroliniana*	Carolina fimbry
Cyperales	Cyperaceae	*Rhynchospora colorata*	starrush whitetop
Cyperales	Cyperaceae	*Schoenoplectus americanus*	American bulrush, chairmaker's bulrush, Olney bulrush
Cyperales	Cyperaceae	*Scleria verticillata*	low nutrush
Polypodiales	Dennstaedtiaceae	*Pteridium aquilinum*	bracken, bracken fern, brackenfern
Polypodiales	Dryopteridaceae	*Polystichum acrostichoides*	Christmas fern
Ebenales	Ebenaceae	*Diospyros virginiana*	common persimmon, eastern persimmon, Persimmon
Ericales	Ericaceae	*Gaylussacia dumosa*	huckleberry
Ericales	Ericaceae	*Vaccinium arboreum*	farkleberry, tree sparkleberry, tree-huckelberry
Ericales	Ericaceae	*Vaccinium corymbosum*	highbush blueberry
Ericales	Ericaceae	*Vaccinium stamineum*	gooseberry, deerberry
Euphorbiales	Euphorbiaceae	*Chamaesyce polygonifolia*	seaside sandmat, seaside spurge
Euphorbiales	Euphorbiaceae	*Cnidoscolus stimulosus*	finger rot
Euphorbiales	Euphorbiaceae	*Croton punctatus*	gulf croton
Fabales	Fabaceae	*Centrosema virginianum*	butterfly pea
Fabales	Fabaceae	*Strophostyles helvola*	beach pea, wild bean
Fagales	Fagaceae	*Quercus laurifolia*	laurel oak
Fagales	Fagaceae	*Quercus nigra*	water oak
Fagales	Fagaceae	*Quercus virginiana*	live oak
Gentianales	Gentianaceae	*Sabatia calycina*	coastal rose gentian
Gentianales	Gentianaceae	*Sabatia campanulata*	slender rose gentian
Juncales	Juncaceae	*Juncus canadensis*	Canadian rush
Juncales	Juncaceae	*Juncus marginatus*	grassleaf rush
Juncales	Juncaceae	*Juncus roemerianus*	needlegrass rush
Lamiales	Lamiaceae	*Teucrium canadense*	American germander, Canada germander, Canada germander
Laurales	Lauraceae	*Persea borbonia*	redbay
Gentianales	Loganiaceae	*Gelsemium sempervirens*	Carolina jessamine, evening trumpetflower
Myrtales	Lythraceae	*Lythrum lineare*	wand lythrum
Magnoliales	Magnoliaceae	*Magnolia grandiflora*	southern magnolia
Malvales	Malvaceae	*Kosteletzkya virginica*	Virginia saltmarsh mallow, Virginia saltmarsh willow
Myricales	Myricaceae	*Morella cerifera*	wax myrtle, waxmyrtle
Scrophulariales	Oleaceae	*Fraxinus sp.*	ash
Scrophulariales	Oleaceae	*Osmanthus americanus*	devilwood
Myrtales	Onagraceae	*Gaura angustifolia*	southern beeblossom
Myrtales	Onagraceae	*Ludwigia alata*	winged primrose-willow
Myrtales	Onagraceae	*Ludwigia repens*	creeping primrosewillow, creeping primrose-willow, creeping waterpurslane
Myrtales	Onagraceae	*Oenothera biennis*	common evening primrose, common eveningprimrose, common evening-primrose

Table B-1. Continued.

Order	Family	Species	Common Name
Myrtales	Onagraceae	*Oenothera humifusa*	seabeach eveningprimrose, seabeach evening-primrose
Orchidales	Orchidaceae	*Spiranthes vernalis*	spring ladies'-tresses, upland ladiestresses
Polypodiales	Osmundaceae	*Osmunda regalis*	royal fern
Geraniales	Oxalidaceae	*Oxalis stricta*	common yellow oxalis, yellow woodsorrel
Violales	Passifloraceae	*Passiflora lutea*	passionflower, yellow passionflower
Caryophyllales	Phytolaccaceae	*Phytolacca americana*	American pokeweed, common pokeweed, inkberry
Pinales	Pinaceae	*Pinus taeda*	loblolly pine
Cyperales	Poaceae	*Andropogon glomeratus*	bushy bluestem
Cyperales	Poaceae	*Cenchrus tribuloides*	sanddune sandbur
Cyperales	Poaceae	*Chasmanthium laxum*	Indian woodoats
Cyperales	Poaceae	*Distichlis spicata*	desert saltgrass, inland saltgrass, marsh spikegrass
Cyperales	Poaceae	*Elymus virginicus*	Virginia wild rye, Virginia wildrye
Cyperales	Poaceae	*Eremochloa ophiuroides*	centipede grass
Cyperales	Poaceae	*Eustachys petraea*	pinewoods fingergrass
Cyperales	Poaceae	*Melica mutica*	oniongrass, twoflower melic, twoflower melicgrass
Cyperales	Poaceae	*Muhlenbergia capillaris*	hairawn muhly
Cyperales	Poaceae	*Panicum amarum*	bitter panicgrass, bitter panicum
Cyperales	Poaceae	*Paspalum urvillei*	Vasey grass, vaseygrass, Vasey's grass
Cyperales	Poaceae	*Paspalum vaginatum*	seashore paspalum
Cyperales	Poaceae	*Phragmites australis*	common reed
Cyperales	Poaceae	*Schizachyrium littorale*	shore little bluestem
Cyperales	Poaceae	*Setaria magna*	giant bristlegrass
Cyperales	Poaceae	*Setaria parviflora*	knotroot bristlegrass, marsh bristle grass, marsh bristlegrass
Cyperales	Poaceae	*Spartina patens*	marshhay cordgrass, salt meadow cordgrass, saltmeadow cordgrass
Cyperales	Poaceae	*Sporobolus virginicus*	seashore dropseed
Cyperales	Poaceae	*Uniola paniculata*	seaoats
Polygonales	Polygonaceae	*Polygonum punctatum*	dotted smartweed
Rhamnales	Rhamnaceae	*Berchemia scandens*	Alabama supplejack
Rosales	Rosaceae	*Potentilla canadensis*	dwarf cinquefoil
Rosales	Rosaceae	*Rosa multiflora*	multiflora rose
Rosales	Rosaceae	*Rosa palustris*	swamp rose
Rosales	Rosaceae	*Rubus cuneifolius*	sand blackberry
Rosales	Rosaceae	*Rubus trivialis*	southern dewberry
Rubiales	Rubiaceae	*Diodia teres*	poor joe, poorjoe, rough buttonweed
Rubiales	Rubiaceae	*Diodia virginiana*	Virginia buttonweed
Rubiales	Rubiaceae	*Galium hispidulum*	coastal bedstraw
Rubiales	Rubiaceae	*Galium obtusum*	bluntleaf bedstraw, blunt-leaf bedstraw, bristly bedstraw
Rubiales	Rubiaceae	*Galium pilosum*	hairy bedstraw
Rubiales	Rubiaceae	*Galium tinctorium*	stiff marsh bedstraw
Rubiales	Rubiaceae	*Mitchella repens*	partridgeberry
Scrophulariales	Scrophulariaceae	*Bacopa monnieri*	coastal waterhyssop, herb of grace, herb-of-grace
Liliales	Smilacaceae	*Smilax glauca*	cat greenbrier

Table B-1. Continued.

Order	Family	Species	Common Name
Solanales	Solanaceae	*Physalis viscosa*	grape groundcherry, groundcherry, starhair groundcherry
Polypodiales	Thelypteridaceae	*Thelypteris palustris*	eastern marsh fern, marsh fern, meadow fern
Urticales	Urticaceae	*Boehmeria cylindrica*	smallspike false nettle, small-spike false nettle, smallspike falsenettle
Lamiales	Verbenaceae	*Callicarpa americana*	American beautyberry
Lamiales	Verbenaceae	*Phyla nodiflora*	frog fruit, sawtooth fogfruit, turkey tangle
Rhamnales	Vitaceae	*Ampelopsis arborea*	sweet peppervine
Rhamnales	Vitaceae	*Parthenocissus quinquefolia*	American ivy, fiveleaved ivy, Virginia creeper
Rhamnales	Vitaceae	*Vitis aestivalis*	summer grape
Rhamnales	Vitaceae	*Vitis rotundifolia*	muscadine, muscadine grape

Table B-2. Vascular plant species detected in each macoplot inventory (i.e., within macroplot species composition) at Cape Lookout National Seashore, 2010.

Sampling Location / Macroplot	Scientific Name
1	*Chamaesyce polygonifolia*
1	*Commelina erecta*
1	*Ilex vomitoria*
1	*Ipomoea sp.*
1	*Juniperus virginiana*
1	*Oenothera biennis*
1	*Persea borbonia*
1	*Parthenocissus quinquefolia*
1	*Physalis viscosa*
1	*Rosa multiflora*
1	*Rubus trivialis*
1	*Smilax sp.*
1	*Spartina patens*
1	*Toxicodendron radicans*
1	*Uniola paniculata*
1	*Vitis rotundifolia*
2	*Andropogon glomeratus*
2	*Baccharis halimifolia*
2	*Chamaesyce polygonifolia*
2	*Cirsium sp.*
2	*Cladium jamaicense*
2	*Conyza canadensis*
2	*Cyperus sp.*
2	*Dichanthelium sp.*
2	*Diodia virginiana*
2	*Eleocharis sp.*
2	*Elymus virginicus*
2	*Eustachys petraea*
2	*Fimbrystilis sp.*
2	*Galium sp.*
2	*Hydrocotyle bonariensis*
2	*Ilex vomitoria*
2	*Ipomoea sagittata*
2	*Iva frutescens*
2	*Juncus canadensis*
2	*Juncus roemerianus*
2	*Juniperus virginiana*
2	*Kosteletzkya virginica*
2	*Lactuca canadensis*
2	*Lepidium virginicum*
2	*Lythrum lineare*
2	*Melothria pendula*
2	*Mikania scandens*
2	*Morella cerifera*
2	*Oenothera humifusa*
2	*Oxypolis sp.*
2	*Parthenocissus quinquefolia*
2	*Paspalum vaginatum*
2	*Phyla nodiflora*
2	*Physalis viscosa*
2	*Phytolacca americana*
2	*Polygonum sp.*
2	*Rubus trivialis*
2	*Rubus cuneifolius*

Table B-2. Continued.

Sampling Location / Macroplot	Scientific Name
2	*Scirpus americanus*
2	*Setaria parviflora*
2	*Smilax sp.*
2	*Solidago sempervirens*
2	*Spartina patens*
2	*Toxicodendron radicans*
2	*Typha sp.*
2	*Unknown Asteraceae*
2	*Unknown Poaceae*
3	*Chamaesyce polygonifolia*
3	*Commelina erecta*
3	*Conyza canadensis*
3	*Croton punctatus*
3	*Heterotheca subaxillaris*
3	*Hydrocotyle bonariensis*
3	*Oenothera humifusa*
3	*Opuntia sp.*
3	*Physalis viscosa*
3	*Uniola paniculata*
3	*Unknown Asteraceae*
3	*Unknown Poaceae*
5	*Andropogon glomeratus*
5	*Baccharis angustifolia*
5	*Baccharis halimifolia*
5	*Bacopa monnieri*
5	*Borrichia frutescens*
5	*Cladium jamaicense*
5	*Cynanchum angustifolium*
5	*Distichlis spicata*
5	*Eupatorium capillifolium*
5	*Fimbrystilis sp.*
5	*Hydrocotyle bonariensis*
5	*Iva frutescens*
5	*Juncus canadensis*
5	*Juncus roemerianus*
5	*Juniperus virginiana*
5	*Kosteletzkya virginica*
5	*Lythrum lineare*
5	*Mikania scandens*
5	*Morella cerifera*
5	*Paspalum vaginatum*
5	*Sabatia calycina*
5	*Scleria verticillata*
5	*Setaria parviflora*
5	*Solidago sempervirens*
5	*Solidago sp.*
5	*Spartina patens*
5	*Spiranthes vernalis*
5	*Toxicodendron radicans*
5	*Unknown Dicot Forb*
6	*Ambrosia artemisiifolia*
6	*Baccharis halimifolia*
6	*Cirsium sp.*
6	*Commelina erecta*
6	*Conyza canadensis*

Table B-2. Continued.

Sampling Location / Macroplot	Scientific Name
6	*Cynanchum angustifolium*
6	*Dichanthelium sp.*
6	*Gaillardia pulchella*
6	*Gaura angustifolia*
6	*Hydrocotyle bonariensis*
6	*Ilex vomitoria*
6	*Ipomoea sagittata*
6	*Juncus roemerianus*
6	*Juncus sp.*
6	*Lepidium virginicum*
6	*Morella cerifera*
6	*Oenothera humifusa*
6	*Opuntia sp.*
6	*Parthenocissus quinquefolia*
6	*Physalis viscosa*
6	*Rubus trivialis*
6	*Schizachyrium sp.*
6	*Smilax sp.*
6	*Solidago sempervirens*
6	*Solidago sp.*
6	*Spartina patens*
6	*Uniola paniculata*
6	*Unknown Asteraceae*
6	*Unknown Dicot Forb*
6	*Strophostyles helvola*
6	*Unknown Lamiaceae*
7	*Baccharis angustifolia*
7	*Baccharis halimifolia*
7	*Chamaesyce polygonifolia*
7	*Commelina erecta*
7	*Conyza canadensis*
7	*Heterotheca subaxillaris*
7	*Hydrocotyle bonariensis*
7	*Morella cerifera*
7	*Oenothera humifusa*
7	*Panicum amarum*
7	*Physalis viscosa*
7	*Scirpus americanus*
7	*Smilax sp.*
7	*Solidago sempervirens*
7	*Spartina patens*
7	*Uniola paniculata*
7	*Unknown Asteraceae*
7	*Strophostyles helvola*
8	*Chamaesyce polygonifolia*
8	*Commelina erecta*
8	*Conyza canadensis*
8	*Diodia teres*
8	*Eremochloa ophiuroides*
8	*Eustachys petraea*
8	*Heterotheca subaxillaris*
8	*Hydrocotyle bonariensis*
8	*Juncus roemerianus*
8	*Juncus sp.*
8	*Juniperus virginiana*

Table B-2. Continued.

Sampling Location / Macroplot	Scientific Name
8	*Morella cerifera*
8	*Oenothera humifusa*
8	*Panicum amarum*
8	*Phyla nodiflora*
8	*Pluchea rosea*
8	*Rhynchospora colorata*
8	*Rhynchospora sp.*
8	*Sabatia sp.*
8	*Spartina patens*
8	*Uniola paniculata*
8	*Unknown Dicot Forb*
8	*Unknown Poaceae*
10	*Andropogon glomeratus*
10	*Baccharis angustifolia*
10	*Baccharis halimifolia*
10	*Borrichia frutescens*
10	*Campsis radicans*
10	*Chamaesyce polygonifolia*
10	*Cirsium sp.*
10	*Cladium jamaicense*
10	*Commelina erecta*
10	*Conyza canadensis*
10	*Cynanchum angustifolium*
10	*Dichanthelium sp.*
10	*Eleocharis sp.*
10	*Elymus virginicus*
10	*Fraxinus caroliniana*
10	*Hydrocotyle bonariensis*
10	*Ilex vomitoria*
10	*Ipomoea sagittata*
10	*Iva frutescens*
10	*Juncus roemerianus*
10	*Juniperus virginiana*
10	*Kosteletzkya virginica*
10	*Lythrum lineare*
10	*Melothria pendula*
10	*Mikania scandens*
10	*Morella cerifera*
10	*Oenothera humifusa*
10	*Osmunda regalis*
10	*Oxalis stricta*
10	*Panicum sp.*
10	*Parthenocissus quinquefolia*
10	*Paspalum urvillei*
10	*Phyla nodiflora*
10	*Physalis viscosa*
10	*Phytolacca americana*
10	*Rhynchospora colorata*
10	*Rubus cuneifolius*
10	*Rubus trivialis*
10	*Scirpus americanus*
10	*Solidago sempervirens*
10	*Spartina patens*
10	*Teucrium canadense*
10	*Toxicodendron radicans*

Table B-2. Continued.

Sampling Location / Macroplot	Scientific Name
10	*Strophostyles helvola*
10	*Unknown Cyperaceae*
10	*Unknown Poaceae*
11	*Ambrosia artemisiifolia*
11	*Ampelopsis arborea*
11	*Baccharis halimifolia*
11	*Borrichia frutescens*
11	*Campsis radicans*
11	*Chamaesyce polygonifolia*
11	*Cirsium horridulum*
11	*Commelina erecta*
11	*Conyza canadensis*
11	*Cynanchum angustifolium*
11	*Cynanchum angustifolium*
11	*Diodia teres*
11	*Elymus virginicus*
11	*Eustachys petraea*
11	*Gaillardia pulchella*
11	*Gaura angustifolia*
11	*Heterotheca subaxillaris*
11	*Hydrocotyle bonariensis*
11	*Ilex vomitoria*
11	*Ipomoea sagittata*
11	*Lepidium virginicum*
11	*Mikania scandens*
11	*Morella cerifera*
11	*Oenothera humifusa*
11	*Panicum amarum*
11	*Physalis viscosa*
11	*Rubus cuneifolius*
11	*Rubus trivialis*
11	*Smilax sp.*
11	*Solidago sempervirens*
11	*Spartina patens*
11	*Uniola paniculata*
11	*Strophostyles helvola*
11	*Vitis rotundifolia*
12	*Ampelopsis arborea*
12	*Baccharis halimifolia*
12	*Chamaesyce polygonifolia*
12	*Commelina erecta*
12	*Conyza canadensis*
12	*Croton punctatus*
12	*Diodia teres*
12	*Eleocharis sp.*
12	*Eremochloa ophiuroides*
12	*Eustachys petraea*
12	*Hydrocotyle bonariensis*
12	*Juncus sp.*
12	*Juniperus virginiana*
12	*Oenothera humifusa*
12	*Opuntia sp.*
12	*Physalis viscosa*
12	*Plantago sp.*
12	*Rhynchospora sp.*

Table B-2. Continued.

Sampling Location / Macroplot	Scientific Name
12	*Rubus sp.*
12	*Sabatia sp.*
12	*Smilax sp.*
12	*Uniola paniculata*
12	*Unknown Asteraceae*
13	*Chamaesyce polygonifolia*
13	*Commelina erecta*
13	*Conyza canadensis*
13	*Croton punctatus*
13	*Gaillardia pulchella*
13	*Heterotheca subaxillaris*
13	*Hydrocotyle bonariensis*
13	*Oenothera humifusa*
13	*Panicum amarum*
13	*Physalis viscosa*
13	*Spartina patens*
13	*Uniola paniculata*
13	*Strophostyles helvola*
14	*Baccharis halimifolia*
14	*Bacopa monnieri*
14	*Borrichia frutescens*
14	*Cynanchum angustifolium*
14	*Cyperus sp.*
14	*Distichlis spicata*
14	*Eleocharis sp.*
14	*Erechtites hieraciifolia*
14	*Ilex vomitoria*
14	*Ipomoea sagittata*
14	*Iva frutescens*
14	*Juncus roemerianus*
14	*Juniperus virginiana*
14	*Kosteletzkya virginica*
14	*Melothria pendula*
14	*Mikania scandens*
14	*Morella cerifera*
14	*Paspalum vaginatum*
14	*Phytolacca americana*
14	*Pluchea camphorata*
14	*Ptilimnium capillaceum*
14	*Rubus trivialis*
14	*Scirpus robustus*
14	*Setaria magna*
14	*Setaria parviflora*
14	*Solidago sp.*
14	*Spartina patens*
14	*Toxicodendron radicans*
14	*Unknown Poaceae*
15	*Chamaesyce polygonifolia*
15	*Commelina erecta*
15	*Conyza canadensis*
15	*Croton punctatus*
15	*Cuscuta sp.*
15	*Eremochloa ophiuroides*
15	*Heterotheca subaxillaris*
15	*Hydrocotyle bonariensis*

Table B-2. Continued.

Sampling Location / Macroplot	Scientific Name
15	*Juniperus virginiana*
15	*Oenothera humifusa*
15	*Opuntia sp.*
15	*Physalis viscosa*
15	*Smilax sp.*
15	*Toxicodendron radicans*
15	*Uniola paniculata*
15	*Heterotheca subaxillaris*
15	*Unknown Dicot Forb*
16	*Chamaesyce polygonifolia*
16	*Conyza canadensis*
16	*Croton punctatus*
16	*Diodia teres*
16	*Eremochloa ophiuroides*
16	*Eustachys petraea*
16	*Heterotheca subaxillaris*
16	*Hydrocotyle bonariensis*
16	*Juniperus virginiana*
16	*Oenothera humifusa*
16	*Panicum amarum*
16	*Physalis viscosa*
16	*Sabatia sp.*
16	*Smilax sp.*
16	*Uniola paniculata*
16	*Strophostyles helvola*
17	*Baccharis halimifolia*
17	*Centella asiatica*
17	*Commelina erecta*
17	*Conyza canadensis*
17	*Cynanchum angustifolium*
17	*Diodia virginiana*
17	*Heterotheca subaxillaris*
17	*Hydrocotyle bonariensis*
17	*Ilex vomitoria*
17	*Juncus roemerianus*
17	*Juncus sp.*
17	*Juniperus virginiana*
17	*Magnolia grandiflora*
17	*Morella cerifera*
17	*Oenothera humifusa*
17	*Parthenocissus quinquefolia*
17	*Persea borbonia*
17	*Phyla nodiflora*
17	*Pinus taeda*
17	*Rhynchospora colorata*
17	*Rubus cuneifolius*
17	*Rubus trivialis*
17	*Schizachyrium sp.*
17	*Smilax sp.*
17	*Spartina patens*
17	*Sporobolus virginicus*
17	*Toxicodendron radicans*
17	*Uniola paniculata*
17	*Unknown Poaceae*
17	*Vitis rotundifolia*

Table B-2. Continued.

Sampling Location / Macroplot	Scientific Name
18	*Baccharis halimifolia*
18	*Cenchrus tribuloides*
18	*Chamaesyce polygonifolia*
18	*Commelina erecta*
18	*Conyza canadensis*
18	*Croton punctatus*
18	*Eremochloa ophiuroides*
18	*Hydrocotyle bonariensis*
18	*Oenothera humifusa*
18	*Panicum amarum*
18	*Physalis viscosa*
18	*Sabatia calycina*
18	*Solidago sempervirens*
18	*Spartina patens*
18	*Uniola paniculata*
18	*Unknown Cyperaceae*
19	*Andropogon glomeratus*
19	*Baccharis angustifolia*
19	*Centella asiatica*
19	*Chamaesyce polygonifolia*
19	*Cirsium sp.*
19	*Cladium jamaicense*
19	*Conyza canadensis*
19	*Cynanchum angustifolium*
19	*Elymus virginicus*
19	*Fimbristylis caroliniana*
19	*Hydrocotyle bonariensis*
19	*Ipomoea sagittata*
19	*Juncus canadensis*
19	*Juncus roemerianus*
19	*Juniperus virginiana*
19	*Melothria pendula*
19	*Mikania scandens*
19	*Morella cerifera*
19	*Oenothera humifusa*
19	*Panicum amarum*
19	*Paspalum vaginatum*
19	*Phyla nodiflora*
19	*Physalis viscosa*
19	*Polygonum punctatum*
19	*Rhynchospora colorata*
19	*Sabatia sp.*
19	*Scirpus americanus*
19	*Scirpus sp.*
19	*Setaria parviflora*
19	*Solidago sempervirens*
19	*Spartina patens*
19	*Toxicodendron radicans*
19	*Uniola paniculata*
19	*Unknown Poaceae*
20	*Andropogon glomeratus*
20	*Baccharis angustifolia*
20	*Baccharis halimifolia*
20	*Berchemia scandens*
20	*Borrichia frutescens*

Table B-2. Continued.

Sampling Location / Macroplot	Scientific Name
20	*Campsis radicans*
20	*Chamaesyce polygonifolia*
20	*Cirsium horridulum*
20	*Commelina erecta*
20	*Conyza canadensis*
20	*Cynanchum angustifolium*
20	*Elymus virginicus*
20	*Fimbristylis caroliniana*
20	*Heterotheca subaxillaris*
20	*Hydrocotyle bonariensis*
20	*Ilex vomitoria*
20	*Iva frutescens*
20	*Juncus roemerianus*
20	*Juncus sp.*
20	*Juniperus virginiana*
20	*Lythrum lineare*
20	*Mikania scandens*
20	*Morella cerifera*
20	*Oenothera humifusa*
20	*Panicum amarum*
20	*Phyla nodiflora*
20	*Physalis viscosa*
20	*Rubus cuneifolius*
20	*Smilax sp.*
20	*Solidago sempervirens*
20	*Spartina patens*
20	*Toxicodendron radicans*
20	*Uniola paniculata*
20	*Strophostyles helvola*
21	*Baccharis angustifolia*
21	*Baccharis halimifolia*
21	*Berchemia scandens*
21	*Cirsium sp.*
21	*Commelina erecta*
21	*Conyza canadensis*
21	*Cynanchum angustifolium*
21	*Gaillardia pulchella*
21	*Heterotheca subaxillaris*
21	*Hydrocotyle bonariensis*
21	*Ilex vomitoria*
21	*Ipomoea sagittata*
21	*Juncus roemerianus*
21	*Juncus sp.*
21	*Juniperus virginiana*
21	*Lythrum lineare*
21	*Mikania scandens*
21	*Morella cerifera*
21	*Oenothera humifusa*
21	*Opuntia sp.*
21	*Parthenocissus quinquefolia*
21	*Persea borbonia*
21	*Phyla nodiflora*
21	*Physalis viscosa*
21	*Plantago sp.*
21	*Rhynchospora colorata*

Table B-2. Continued.

Sampling Location / Macroplot	Scientific Name
21	*Rubus trivialis*
21	*Sabatia sp.*
21	*Schizachyrium sp.*
21	*Scirpus americanus*
21	*Smilax sp.*
21	*Solidago sempervirens*
21	*Solidago sp.*
21	*Spartina patens*
21	*Toxicodendron radicans*
21	*Uniola paniculata*
22	*Baccharis halimifolia*
22	*Borrichia frutescens*
22	*Centrosema virginianum*
22	*Cynanchum angustifolium*
22	*Elymus virginicus*
22	*Ilex vomitoria*
22	*Ipomoea sagittata*
22	*Iva frutescens*
22	*Juncus roemerianus*
22	*Juniperus virginiana*
22	*Lythrum lineare*
22	*Melica mutica*
22	*Morella cerifera*
22	*Panicum sp.*
22	*Parthenocissus quinquefolia*
22	*Paspalum vaginatum*
22	*Phytolacca americana*
22	*Rubus cuneifolius*
22	*Rubus trivialis*
22	*Setaria parviflora*
22	*Smilax glauca*
22	*Solidago sempervirens*
22	*Spartina patens*
22	*Toxicodendron radicans*
22	*Unknown Fabaceae*
22	*Unknown Poaceae*
22	*Vitis rotundifolia*
23	*Ambrosia artemisiifolia*
23	*Ampelopsis arborea*
23	*Andropogon glomeratus*
23	*Argemone sp.*
23	*Baccharis angustifolia*
23	*Baccharis halimifolia*
23	*Borrichia frutescens*
23	*Campsis radicans*
23	*Centella asiatica*
23	*Centrosema virginianum*
23	*Commelina erecta*
23	*Cynanchum angustifolium*
23	*Diospyros virginiana*
23	*Elymus virginicus*
23	*Gaillardia pulchella*
23	*Galium hispidulum*
23	*Heterotheca subaxillaris*
23	*Hydrocotyle bonariensis*

Sampling Location / Macroplot	Scientific Name
23	*Ilex vomitoria*
23	*Ipomoea sagittata*
23	*Iva frutescens*
23	*Juncus roemerianus*
23	*Juniperus virginiana*
23	*Kosteletzkya virginica*
23	*Lactuca sp.*
23	*Lythrum lineare*
23	*Mikania scandens*
23	*Morella cerifera*
23	*Oenothera humifusa*
23	*Opuntia sp.*
23	*Parthenocissus quinquefolia*
23	*Phyla nodiflora*
23	*Physalis viscosa*
23	*Rhynchospora colorata*
23	*Rosa palustris*
23	*Setaria magna*
23	*Smilax sp.*
23	*Solidago sp.*
23	*Spartina patens*
23	*Toxicodendron radicans*
23	*Typha sp.*
23	*Uniola paniculata*
23	*Unknown Cyperaceae*
23	*Strophostyles helvola*
24	*Ambrosia artemisiifolia*
24	*Ampelopsis arborea*
24	*Asclepias sp.*
24	*Asplenium platyneuron*
24	*Berchemia scandens*
24	*Boehmeria cylindrica*
24	*Callicarpa americana*
24	*Carpinus caroliniana*
24	*Centella asiatica*
24	*Chasmanthium laxum*
24	*Cnidoscolus stimulosus*
24	*Cornus foemina*
24	*Cyperus haspan*
24	*Desmodium sp.*
24	*Diodia virginiana*
24	*Diospyros virginiana*
24	*Eleocharis sp.*
24	*Elephantopus tomentosus*
24	*Galium obtusum*
24	*Galium pilosum*
24	*Hibiscus sp.*
24	*Hydrocotyle bonariensis*
24	*Hypericum hypericoides*
24	*Ilex opaca*
24	*Ilex vomitoria*
24	*Ipomoea sagittata*
24	*Juncus marginatus*
24	*Juncus roemerianus*
24	*Juniperus virginiana*

Table B-2. Continued.

Sampling Location / Macroplot	Scientific Name
24	*Kosteletzkya virginica*
24	*Ludwigia repens*
24	*Magnolia grandiflora*
24	*Mikania scandens*
24	*Mitchella repens*
24	*Morella cerifera*
24	*Osmanthus americanus*
24	*Osmunda regalis*
24	*Panicum sp.*
24	*Parthenocissus quinquefolia*
24	*Passiflora lutea*
24	*Phyla nodiflora*
24	*Pinus taeda*
24	*Pluchea rosea*
24	*Polygonum sp.*
24	*Polystichum acrostichoides*
24	*Potentilla canadensis*
24	*Quercus laurifolia*
24	*Quercus nigra*
24	*Quercus virginiana*
24	*Rhynchospora colorata*
24	*Rhynchospora sp.*
24	*Rosa palustris*
24	*Rubus sp.*
24	*Rubus trivialis*
24	*Sabatia campanulata*
24	*Sanicula canadensis*
24	*Scirpus americanus*
24	*Smilax sp.*
24	*Thelypteris palustris*
24	*Toxicodendron radicans*
24	*Typha sp.*
24	*Unknown Asteraceae*
24	*Unknown Cyperaceae*
24	*Unknown Dicot Forb*
24	*Unknown Fabaceae*
24	*Unknown Fern*
24	*Unknown Poaceae*
24	*Vaccinium corymbosum*
24	*Vitis aestivalis*
24	*Vitis rotundifolia*
25	*Andropogon glomeratus*
25	*Chamaesyce polygonifolia*
25	*Commelina erecta*
25	*Conyza canadensis*
25	*Croton punctatus*
25	*Fimbristylis caroliniana*
25	*Hydrocotyle bonariensis*
25	*Juncus canadensis*
25	*Juncus marginatus*
25	*Mikania scandens*
25	*Morella cerifera*
25	*Oenothera humifusa*
25	*Rhynchospora sp.*
25	*Scleria verticillata*

Table B-2. Continued.

Sampling Location / Macroplot	Scientific Name
25	*Solidago sempervirens*
25	*Spartina patens*
25	*Spiranthes sp.*
25	*Uniola paniculata*
25	*Unknown Cyperaceae*
25	*Unknown Poaceae*
26	*Chamaesyce polygonifolia*
26	*Commelina erecta*
26	*Croton punctatus*
26	*Heterotheca subaxillaris*
26	*Hydrocotyle bonariensis*
26	*Oenothera humifusa*
26	*Opuntia humifusa*
26	*Physalis viscosa*
26	*Spartina patens*
26	*Uniola paniculata*
27	*Ampelopsis arborea*
27	*Chamaecrista sp.*
27	*Cnidoscolus stimulosus*
27	*Elephantopus tomentosus*
27	*Eremochloa ophiuroides*
27	*Eupatorium capillifolium*
27	*Gaylussacia dumosa*
27	*Gelsemium sempervirens*
27	*Hydrocotyle umbellata*
27	*Ilex glabra*
27	*Ilex opaca*
27	*Juniperus virginiana*
27	*Morella cerifera*
27	*Osmanthus americanus*
27	*Parthenocissus quinquefolia*
27	*Persea borbonia*
27	*Pinus taeda*
27	*Pteridium aquilinum*
27	*Quercus laurifolia*
27	*Quercus virginiana*
27	*Rhus copallinum*
27	*Smilax sp.*
27	*Solidago sp.*
27	*Toxicodendron radicans*
27	*Unknown Asteraceae*
27	*Vaccinium arboreum*
27	*Vaccinium stamineum*
27	*Vitis rotundifolia*
27	*Yucca aloifolia*
27	*Yucca gloriosa*
28	*Andropogon glomeratus*
28	*Baccharis angustifolia*
28	*Chamaesyce polygonifolia*
28	*Cirsium horridulum*
28	*Commelina erecta*
28	*Conyza canadensis*
28	*Croton punctatus*
28	*Diodia teres*
28	*Elymus virginicus*

Table B-2. Continued.

Sampling Location / Macroplot	Scientific Name
28	*Eustachys petraea*
28	*Gaillardia pulchella*
28	*Heterotheca subaxillaris*
28	*Hydrocotyle bonariensis*
28	*Iva frutescens*
28	*Juncus canadensis*
28	*Juniperus virginiana*
28	*Morella cerifera*
28	*Muhlenbergia capillaris*
28	*Oenothera humifusa*
28	*Opuntia humifusa*
28	*Panicum sp.*
28	*Parthenocissus quinquefolia*
28	*Phyla nodiflora*
28	*Physalis viscosa*
28	*Plantago sp.*
28	*Sabatia calycina*
28	*Schizachyrium littorale*
28	*Solidago sempervirens*
28	*Spartina patens*
28	*Toxicodendron radicans*
28	*Uniola paniculata*
28	*Strophostyles helvola*
28	*Unknown Poaceae*
29	*Andropogon glomeratus*
29	*Baccharis angustifolia*
29	*Baccharis halimifolia*
29	*Borrichia frutescens*
29	*Cladium jamaicense*
29	*Commelina erecta*
29	*Conyza canadensis*
29	*Cynanchum angustifolium*
29	*Cyperus sp.*
29	*Elymus virginicus*
29	*Eupatorium capillifolium*
29	*Fimbristylis sp.*
29	*Fimbristylis caroliniana*
29	*Hydrocotyle bonariensis*
29	*Ilex vomitoria*
29	*Ipomoea sagittata*
29	*Iva frutescens*
29	*Juncus canadensis*
29	*Juncus roemerianus*
29	*Juniperus virginiana*
29	*Kosteletzkya virginica*
29	*Lepidium virginicum*
29	*Melothria pendula*
29	*Mikania scandens*
29	*Morella cerifera*
29	*Oenothera humifusa*
29	*Paspalum vaginatum*
29	*Physalis viscosa*
29	*Phytolacca americana*
29	*Rubus trivialis*
29	*Sabatia calycina*

Table B-2. Continued.

Sampling Location / Macroplot	Scientific Name
29	*Scirpus americanus*
29	*Scirpus robustus*
29	*Setaria parviflora*
29	*Solidago sempervirens*
29	*Spartina patens*
29	*Spiranthes vernalis*
29	*Toxicodendron radicans*
29	*Typha sp.*
29	*Unknown Cyperaceae*
30	*Ampelopsis arborea*
30	*Andropogon glomeratus*
30	*Baccharis angustifolia*
30	*Baccharis halimifolia*
30	*Borrichia frutescens*
30	*Commelina erecta*
30	*Cynanchum angustifolium*
30	*Hydrocotyle bonariensis*
30	*Ilex vomitoria*
30	*Ipomoea sagittata*
30	*Iva frutescens*
30	*Juncus roemerianus*
30	*Juniperus virginiana*
30	*Kosteletzkya virginica*
30	*Lythrum lineare*
30	*Morella cerifera*
30	*Sabatia sp.*
30	*Smilax sp.*
30	*Solidago sempervirens*
30	*Spartina patens*
30	*Toxicodendron radicans*
30	*Elymus virginicus*
30	*Unknown Poaceae*
30	*Vitis rotundifolia*
Alt 01	*Chamaesyce polygonifolia*
Alt 01	*Cirsium horridulum*
Alt 01	*Conyza canadensis*
Alt 01	*Heterotheca subaxillaris*
Alt 01	*Hydrocotyle bonariensis*
Alt 01	*Morella cerifera*
Alt 01	*Oenothera humifusa*
Alt 01	*Solidago sempervirens*
Alt 01	*Spartina patens*
Alt 01	*Uniola paniculata*
Alt 01	*Strophostyles helvola*
Alt 02	*Baccharis halimifolia*
Alt 02	*Chamaesyce polygonifolia*
Alt 02	*Commelina erecta*
Alt 02	*Conyza canadensis*
Alt 02	*Croton punctatus*
Alt 02	*Cynanchum angustifolium*
Alt 02	*Cyperus sp.*
Alt 02	*Erechtites hieraciifolia*
Alt 02	*Galium tinctorium*
Alt 02	*Heterotheca subaxillaris*
Alt 02	*Hydrocotyle bonariensis*

Table B-2. Continued.

Sampling Location / Macroplot	Scientific Name
Alt 02	*Ilex vomitoria*
Alt 02	*Juncus roemerianus*
Alt 02	*Juniperus virginiana*
Alt 02	*Lepidium virginicum*
Alt 02	*Ludwigia alata*
Alt 02	*Ludwigia sp.*
Alt 02	*Lythrum lineare*
Alt 02	*Melothria pendula*
Alt 02	*Mikania scandens*
Alt 02	*Morella cerifera*
Alt 02	*Oenothera humifusa*
Alt 02	*Panicum amarum*
Alt 02	*Panicum sp.*
Alt 02	*Parthenocissus quinquefolia*
Alt 02	*Persea borbonia*
Alt 02	*Phragmites australis*
Alt 02	*Phyla nodiflora*
Alt 02	*Polygonum sp.*
Alt 02	*Ptilimnium capillaceum*
Alt 02	*Rhynchospora colorata*
Alt 02	*Rhynchospora sp.*
Alt 02	*Rosa multiflora*
Alt 02	*Rubus cuneifolius*
Alt 02	*Rubus trivialis*
Alt 02	*Schizachyrium littorale*
Alt 02	*Smilax sp.*
Alt 02	*Solidago sempervirens*
Alt 02	*Solidago sp.*
Alt 02	*Spartina patens*
Alt 02	*Toxicodendron radicans*
Alt 02	*Uniola paniculata*
Alt 02	*Vitis rotundifolia*